The Mythic Guide to Characters

Writing Characters Who Enchant and Inspire

Antonio del Drago

Edited by Derek Bowen

ISBN: 0615752314
ISBN-13: 978-0615752310

This book is dedicated to

MY FAVORITE GEEK

CONTENTS

Getting Started

There's no one right way to create a character. What this guide offers is one possible approach that's designed to help you, the author, explore possibilities that wouldn't have occurred to you otherwise. The end result will, hopefully, be a richer writing experience, and characters who will enchant and inspire your readers.

The steps outlined in this guide are not absolutely necessary in order to write a good book. But the tools that you'll gain here can certainly *help* you to reach that goal with greater clarity and confidence.

So, what does this book offer that can help writers? Primarily, we'll be exploring the rudiments of mind and behavior that shape all human actions.

Readers are drawn to characters who make them feel something. They want to root for the hero to succeed. They want to feel genuine love and appreciation for the hero's allies. They want to feel apprehension and anger towards the villain. To spur these feelings, your characters must be realistic. You must write them as if they are real people.

Having an understanding of how the mind works will greatly help you in this endeavor. It should be stressed that the human mind is exceedingly complex. It's responsible for much of the good and evil that has befallen this world. The mind both builds and destroys entire societies. It has supplied the brilliance to cure diseases, and has developed the horrors of modern warfare. It's perhaps the most intricate and unpredictable thing in our known universe.

This book doesn't presume to tell you *exactly* how the mind works. I won't lie and tell you that a specific type of person can *always* be expected to react in a certain way when confronted with a specific situation. Indeed, a person who always reacts in a perfectly predictable fashion is too shallow to be credible: no real person is like that. On the other hand, a person who demonstrates no clear pattern of reactions is equally unbelievable.

What I will tell you is that with a general understanding of how the brain works, you can determine the most *likely* category a type of person falls into, and the most *likely* way that person will interact with different scenarios. Knowing this will give you a richer understanding of who your characters are, and how they should act within the world you choose to place them in.

This guide approaches the art of character creation in three layers.

The first and deepest layer is the character's unconscious mind, which forms the basis of his actions and motivations.

The second layer is how the character relates to his or her world. This includes how the character approaches the world, and the character's formative relationships.

The third and final layer is the character's role in your story. This layer can be developed using mythological archetypes, as well as a concept known as the Soul Triptych.

This approach to character development may seem complex, but it will result in compelling, multidimensional characters. Two-dimensional characters are easy to produce. *Good* characters take work and practice to build.

That being said, let's start building. ·

Layer 1: The Character Within

The Unconscious Mind

The first layer involves the innermost workings of your character's mind. Because it's the foundation of who he is as a person, it will impact all of your character's other attributes.

Most of our actions are guided by our unconscious mind, which is sometimes referred to as the "subconscious." Because it drives so many of our choices, having an understanding of the unconscious mind is crucial when developing realistic characters. If you have knowledge of the conscious mind vs. the unconscious mind, you'll realize that your character isn't going to make exclusively sound and well-thought out decisions. Instead, you'll realize that much of his behavior is guided by impulse.

When first being introduced to the concept of the unconscious mind, a useful metaphor is an iceberg. The tip of the iceberg is all that we can see, floating above the surface of the water. The far greater portion of the iceberg is submerged and out of sight. The smaller portion, the part we see, is the conscious mind. It contains the thoughts and memories that we're presently aware of. The greater portion of the iceberg, the part we cannot see, is the unconscious mind. It holds memories, drives and instincts that aren't currently in use.

What's the name of the town that you were born in? The answer probably came to you right away. But from where did the answer come? Surely you weren't sitting there thinking "I was born in 'X'" all day. The thought was nowhere in your head until you were asked for it. Or was it? The knowledge of where you were born was being stored in your unconscious mind.

The conscious mind can hold only so much within it at a given time. Memories are stored within the unconscious mind, and the conscious mind reaches inside to retrieve them. But it should be noted that the unconscious mind is very, very deep. Not all of it can be summoned on a whim.

Have you ever had a hard time remembering someone's name? Perhaps this was an old friend from high school? No matter how hard you try, the answer may not come to you. But say you were given a sheet of paper with four names on it. These names are all different, and one of them is the name of your friend. Would you recognize the name when you saw it? Probably, yes. Why is that? Obviously the memory was still in your mind *somewhere* if you were able to access it with the help of a little stimulation. So why couldn't you just conjure it at will?

Some memories are pushed down deeper than others. If you haven't pulled a particular memory into your conscious mind in a long while, it could slink further and further into your unconscious mind. It's still in there somewhere, but it is harder to access. In severe circumstances, such as mental illness or brain trauma, a person may develop a suppressed memory. This is a memory shoved so far into the "basement" of the unconscious mind that it may never be pulled back into the conscious mind ever again. But just because it's been shut away doesn't mean that it won't affect that person's behavior.

Elements of the unconscious that aren't currently in play within the conscious mind can *still* influence your actions. Say there was a certain cartoon that you loved when you were three years old. You laughed and felt happy whenever you watched it. Now let's say that you are shopping for groceries today, and come across a new breakfast cereal. You decide to buy it.

This could be because the cartoon character on the box shares similarities with the main character of that childhood cartoon. The thought may not even come into your conscious mind: "Hey! This mascot reminds me of Captain Awesome!" You may not even remember who Captain Awesome was, young as you were when you watched his show.

But the unconscious memory of him still triggers a response in your behavior. It influenced you to buy a brand of cereal you otherwise might not have.

The unconscious mind also contains more than just memories. Most of your brain activity takes place within it. If you're walking down the street, and suddenly a ball flies towards you, you may duck, flinch, or raise your hands to protect your face. Now, in the split second that you saw the ball flying at you in the corner of your eye, you didn't use logic to determine "Oh, look, a flying projectile. I should execute a defensive maneuver so as to minimize my chances of injury." Instead, you just reacted without a thought in your mind, beyond perhaps "AHH!"

For that matter, consider how much is going on in the background in the simple act of walking. If you think this is trivial, try walking while thinking out every single movement of every muscle you use in the process. If you're fond of falling on your face, try running while doing this.

Even when given proper time to think, our unconscious can still heavily influence the conscious mind. A lot of people stay in relationships with people they hate. Their conscious mind is logically thinking, "Look, you're not *happy* anymore. You're giving and giving, and getting nothing back. They don't listen to you, they don't *care* about you. It's time to move on. It will be hard at first, but your life will be better in the long run because of it."

And yet... it's rarely that simple, is it? That's because our unconscious mind is still thinking, "You'll end up alone. You'll probably die alone. It's your fault that you couldn't get this relationship to work. You're the one quitting, after all. You loved them once. You could love them again. A part of you *still* loves them. If you leave now, then it was all for nothing. You *wasted* those years if you leave now." Of course, the unconscious mind is not articulating these thoughts in such a fashion. Rather, these thoughts will manifest themselves as raw emotions. But they'll be there.

Even if you *do* take these unconscious thoughts into your conscious mind, analyze them, and determine that they are misguided, they may *still* keep you from leaving the person you no longer love. You can shut the negative thoughts out of your conscious mind, but they're still alive in your unconscious.

The unconscious mind can make us do the wrong thing against our better judgment. It can even make us do the *right* thing against our better judgment. Say you want to leave the person you're with for the *wrong* reasons. Say you want to leave because your conscious mind is telling you that you still have things you want to do before you get married. There are places you want to travel, exciting and maybe even dangerous things you want to do. The thought of dedicating yourself to just one person for the rest of your life may scare you. But against the "logical" part of your brain, for reasons you can't articulate, you love that person. And that simple argument, "I love him," trumps your conscious protests… in this case, to the good.

You can see how being aware of these elements would impact your writing in a romance novel (or any novel, for that matter). Understand that your characters aren't always going to do what's best for them. They're not always going to do what would be their choice, were they thinking logically. And even when they *are* using logic, those thoughts are still being guided by the unconscious.

Even if you *want* your character to be with a certain person, you have to ask yourself if the character you've established *would* be with that person.

Let's say Shakespeare came to love Juliet as a character. As he wrote his timeless classic, perhaps when Juliet awoke to find Romeo dead, the thought may have crossed Shakespeare's mind that Juliet could weep and cry, but move on. She could have, in all logical sense, slowly picked up the pieces of her life and found someone else. And then the story would have faded into obscurity and died.

Romeo and Juliet acted on impulses. They chose to be with people that they knew their families wouldn't approve of, then took drastic measures when their efforts to be together kept failing. The families, too, were acting on unconscious motivations. Neither side remembered how their feud started, but from a young age they had all been taught to respond with hatred and anger at the sight of their rivals. Reasons did not matter: the feud was all.

Romeo and Juliet could have even been guided by unconscious motives that we, the readers, are not made aware of. Perhaps Juliet shared a facial structure with a woman that Romeo saw when he was younger, who gave him his first rush of sexual desire. He didn't know what that feeling was at the time, and may not even remember seeing this woman. But those facial features became fixed in his unconscious, and formed the foundation for what he automatically perceives as the "ideal" woman. Or maybe, to take the Oedipal view, Juliet reminded him of his mother.

The same could be said for Juliet. Perhaps Romeo wore an outfit when they first met that was similar in style to an outfit worn by a street vendor who gave Juliet flowers when she was little. She sees Romeo and has stirrings of kindness fluttering inside her.

Some authors claim that they don't control their characters or their plotlines: that they merely "observe" what happens in their own minds, and then write it down.

I would say that this is a half-truth. You control what you choose to write about, who your characters are, and how you want your plotlines to flow. But a novel is like a house of cards—indeed, like *any* piece of architecture, no matter what materials are used in its construction. As you continue to build, there are certain rules that you have to follow. Place too much weight in an area where it doesn't belong, and it falls apart. The same is true when building a novel from the ground up to adhere to a certain "structure," and then making a character act in a way that she wouldn't. You either have to let her make her own choices, or start all over in order to change who she is as a person.

Once you've established who a character is at her core, you have to remain true to that knowledge in order to preserve your novel's integrity. When a character is faced with a hard decision, ask yourself honestly what the character would do, not what you would *want* her to do, or what you hope *you* would do if faced with the same choice. Is she going to make a wrong choice every now and then? Is she going to make mistakes and perhaps pay for them later? If you're a good writer, then the answers are probably "yes."

This is the true half in the claim above. Authors often discuss this in terms of characters "doing things that surprise" the author. That is, once the character becomes a real, three-dimensional person for the author, the author finds that the character cannot be "forced" to do things that are contrary to the personality he's established... not even if he *needs* the character to do something in order to advance the plot. Good writers will respect this, and find alternative ways to accomplish the same goal. Those who do not end up with characters that sound implausible at best, if not outright contrived.

Now, this may raise some difficulties for you, especially if you're still new to the writing game. How, exactly, are you supposed to know how your character will act in any given situation?

How do you determine who they are as people?

Don't underestimate your power as the omniscient creator of these characters. You have access to memories that they have long forgotten, and you can determine why and how they feel a certain way. As the creator, you can provide them with these memories whenever you need to motivate a certain course of action—at least to the extent that these don't blatantly contradict something you've already established. Such emendations need to account for why the character is acting in a certain way in *present* circumstances as well as why she does *not* do so in other, seemingly similar ones. (Or perhaps she would have: revision is not a crime.)

If this seems overwhelming, don't worry. The next chapter will help you to determine "who" your character is through means of the enneagram.

The Enneagram

The Enneagram of Personality, which is commonly referred to as simply the "enneagram," is a tool used to explore personality types. It does so by classifying individuals into nine categories based on their unconscious drives and motivations. (The term itself is formed from the Greek "ennea," nine, plus "grammos," something written or drawn.) Writers can use the enneagram to help develop the unconscious minds of their characters, which is the deepest layer of character building. When used effectively, the enneagram can add depth and realism.

The enneagram itself has an interesting history. Its proponents believe that its principles first originated with Evagrius of Pontus, a 4th century Christian mystic and author. Other proponents claim that it has roots in Sufi mysticism, although this is disputable. But we do know that it was first introduced to the West by George Gurdjieff (1866-1949), a self-described teacher of "esoteric Christianity."

The enneagram was further advanced by Oscar Ichazo (b. 1931), a Bolivian-born mystic and spiritual teacher. Ichazo is credited with developing the current iteration of the enneagram, with its emphasis on nine personality types.

Most psychologists question the validity of the enneagram as a model of human personality, as it cannot be scientifically verified. It has found popularity, though, as a tool for spiritual growth in religious and New Age circles, as well as in self-help programs.

For our purpose, the scientific validity of the enneagram isn't an issue. After all, we won't be using it for psychological or even spiritual ends. But for us as writers, it's useful as a possible starting point for delineating the unconscious motivations of our characters.

While the enneagram classifies people into types, it still recognizes that no two individuals are alike. Just because two people fall into the same category within the enneagram, it doesn't mean that they will *always* make the same decisions throughout their lives. Nor does it mean that two people in different categories are guaranteed to take dramatically different approaches to life at every turn.

In fact, all human beings exhibit aspects of all nine personality types, although we tend to fit one type more consistently than the others. In *The Enneagram: Understanding Yourself and the Others in Your Life*, author Helen Palmer notes that:

The Enneagram, however, is not a fixed system. It is a model of interconnecting lines that indicate a dynamic movement in which each of us has the potential of all nine positions, although we identify most strongly with the issues of our own type. The structure of a nine-pointed star with interconnecting lines also suggests that each type possesses a versatility of movement between all nine positions.

The enneagram isn't a foolproof way to predict behavior, but it's still a valuable tool. It can be used to determine the most *likely* way that an individual will react when presented with a problem. Odds are that you're already using an approach similar to the enneagram in your daily life, but not in a consciously articulated fashion.

Have you ever generalized someone, such as a friend or family member, by describing him as "easy-going?" You know that if he's faced with something like a flat tire, he'll just shrug it off and go on with his day.

This is how the enneagram works. You determine what kind of "person" the individual is, and this gives you a sense as to how he handles things. The easy-going individual mentioned above could likely fall into the Type 9 personality within the enneagram, "The Peacemaker."

The nine names for the personality types will vary slightly from one source to another. For instance, Type 9, "The Peacemaker" has also been referred to as "The Meditator." While their names can vary and their descriptions can change slightly, the enneagram remains fairly consistent from one source to another.

Each type has its own strengths and weaknesses. Here they are listed in order:

1. The Perfectionist: Perfectionists tends to take morals and ideals very seriously. They seek to do what's right at all costs. In their constant efforts to do what's right, their high ideals can cause clashes with other people. They can give off a "preachy" or even resentful vibe towards people who don't share the same ideals.

2. The Giver: This personality type wishes to help others. They have a great deal of empathy and are eager to lend assistance. Their constant need to help or save others can come across as obsessive. It could be said that they *need* to be *needed*. When there is no need to be met, they may come across as clingy and possessive: "co-dependent," at the extreme end.

3. The Achiever: Individuals who fall under this category have a drive to succeed in all things. This "take no prisoners" attitude can lead to great success, but it can also breed arrogance. Wanting to succeed too badly can sometimes

lead achievers to compromise their morals. In such cases, they may feel that the end justifies the means. Alternately, their drive can be self-destructive, if they allow "take no prisoners" to include themselves.

4. The Romantic: These are extremely passionate people. Romantics are often creative and individualistic; they also often have high degrees of empathy. They can sometimes come across as too emotional. Their hyper emotions can cause them to be likeable when happy, and almost intolerable when sad. Their great dread is being "ordinary" or "normal."

5. The Observer: "Introverted" is a term that might come to mind when describing this personality type. They quietly analyze all situations and rely on logic to solve their problems without looking for help from others. These people can be perceived as detached or aloof, and at their worst as hermits, constantly shutting out the world around them. This is a mistake in others' perceptions: Observers are *keenly* aware of the world around them. It's just that they're frequently not interested in being a *part* of that world... perhaps because of their observations.

6. The Questioner: Questioners are often scrupulous in terms of safety and security. They want to be certain that a course of action is safe

before proceeding. Sometimes this causes them to be voices of reason in a group, but sometimes they appear to be paranoid or downright cowardly. "Skeptic" is another name often applied to this type.

7. The Adventurer: This is the type of person that cannot sit still for very long. Adventurers want to see the world and revel in the experiences that it offers. Their energetic attitude can be fun-loving and likeable, but they can also be impulsive or reckless, and are rarely satisfied to rest on their laurels.

8. The Protector: Protectors want stability and control of the world around them. They desire that everything be kept in order. For this reason, they make good authority figures; "Leader" is another name sometimes applied to this type. At times they can be over-zealous, and may become frustrated when something is beyond their control. At their most negative, they can become obsessed with increasing their own power in order to impose the stability the desire.

9. The Peacemaker: This personality type always seeks for things to go smoothly and easily. They detest conflict and wish that everyone would get along. They can be a calming presence and sometimes excel as mediators. At other times,

their laid back attitude can seem lazy or cowardly.

As has already been stressed, you need to make your characters realistic, allowing them to make their own decisions independent of your own desires. The enneagram is a means of defining the line between your own personality and theirs. It gives you a rudimentary template of who they are, and therefore how they will likely act.

Our personality types are believed to guide our actions. Most human beings seem to follow certain pre-programmed "scripts," which are connected to their enneagram personality types. These types exist primarily in the unconscious mind, yet guide our conscious choices. If someone flies off the handle over a small issue, she didn't make a conscious choice to overreact. Rather, her unconscious identity might be assigned to the Type 8 personality, and an inability to control what's going on around her can result in illogical anger because of it.

Again, having a personality type doesn't mean that your "label" will guide your every move. Sometimes a carefree individual can be serious, and sometimes an assertive individual can be laid back. The personality types are based on generalizations of who you are as a whole, how you think and act *most* of the time.

There's also a great degree of variety within the personality types. Some people may not fit easily into any one category, as they may have two or three areas that seem to match them.

It should also be noted that enneagram personality types are not the same thing as archetypes, which will be discussed later. In brief, an archetype is a label for a character's role within your story—such as a hero, villain, ally, mentor and so on. Some enneagram personality types fit well within certain archetypes, but they are not directly correlated to each other.

For instance, the Type 1 personality, "The Perfectionist," could work beautifully for both a protagonist and an antagonist. This personality type only indicates that the individual strives to meet her own standards and morals, but it doesn't specify what those morals are. Many villains don't view themselves as evil, and in fact adhere to a strict code of conduct. The fact that the villain's goals are not in the best interest of the protagonist is what sets him apart as an antagonist.

To illustrate how personality types can affect a character, here's a list of well-known literary icons. There's one for each of the nine personality types within the enneagram. This isn't an *official* list by any means. The authors themselves haven't revealed these to be the personality types for their characters, nor were these examples taken from any preexisting list. These examples are strictly based on my own analysis.

We'll be discussing in detail some of the hard choices these characters have made, and the results of those choices. So be warned, there will be spoilers ahead. In fact, this entire book is going to have quite a few spoilers sprinkled here and there.

With that said, let's move on to the list.

1. The Perfectionist: "Harry Potter" from the seven-book series of the same name, by J.K. Rowling

As stated earlier, the Perfectionist has strong principles and ideals. He strives to do what's right as often as he can. I chose Harry Potter as an example of this personality type, as he constantly displays a strong will and a refusal to compromise his principles, even when his own safety is at stake.

In the first book, the antagonist, Lord Voldemort (who murdered Harry's parents) offers to help Harry bring his parents back to life, on the condition that Harry hands over a magical item that he desires. Harry refuses, knowing that such a powerful item shouldn't end up in the hands of someone so evil.

Earlier in the novel, another student who was born into wealth belittles Harry's new friend, Ron. This other student, Draco Malfoy, tells Harry that he'll be more successful if he hangs out with a "better crowd." Essentially, Draco is saying that he'd be a more valuable ally than Ron, and that he's willing to befriend Harry if Harry forsakes Ron. It's true that Draco is a wealthier and better trained wizard than Ron, with powerful family connections. Logically, he would have been the superior choice, but Harry refuses to sell out his principles for gain.

This theme remains consistent throughout the series. Harry stays true to people that he feels are genuine, choosing to associate with social outcasts like Ron, Neville and Luna, even though this invites scorn and rivalry from the popular students.

Even when the going gets tough, Harry never deviates from his moral convictions. In many of the books, Harry breaks the rules of the school in order to do what he feels is right, revealing that he holds his principles in higher regard than prewritten rules. This puts him at odds with authority figures on more than one occasion.

Characters such as this, who'll always do what they consider to be right, no matter what the cost, can often be considered Perfectionist personalities.

2. The Giver: "Samwise Gamgee" from *The Lord of the Rings* trilogy, by J. R. R. Tolkien

The Giver always puts others before himself. No character better fits this personality type than the faithful Samwise, or "Sam," Gamgee. Early in the trilogy, Sam vows to protect the story's protagonist, Frodo Baggins. Throughout their difficult travels, Samwise displays intense loyalty and an eagerness to help, even placing his own life in danger.

Being a hobbit, Sam is small in stature. Yet he stands up to some of the most menacing foes—and sometimes friends—imaginable in order to protect others. One of the most memorable threats he faces is Shelob, a giant spider that poisons Frodo and attempts to eat him. Sam risks his life fighting this creature, all for the sake of defending his friend.

While his protective and caring nature is shown primarily in regards to Frodo, there are other instances of him being selfless. Early in the novel, the band of travelers acquire a malnourished pony. Sam cares for and downright spoils this beast, and is saddened when the pony can no longer accompany them.

He's also fond of singing and storytelling, constantly trying to brighten the spirits of those around him.

Like most Givers, his compassionate nature can sometimes come across as overbearing. On more than one occasion, he's told to stay behind while the others progress forward into unknown dangers. Despite assurances that the roads ahead are no place for the likes of him, he outright demands that he be included so that he can look after Frodo and the others. Even when Frodo tries to continue alone—and succeeds in shaking the rest of the party—Sam correctly intuits the situation and catches up with Frodo... nearly drowning himself in the process.

His overbearing nature is also shown after the reintroduction of Gollum. Ever protective of Frodo, Sam greatly distrusts Gollum and constantly belittles him. This upsets Frodo, but Sam cannot help berating this creature whom he believes intends Frodo harm. The same can be seen, if to a lesser extent, in contacts with others Sam distrusts, such as the humans they interact with along the way. Givers can be expected to offer "help," even when it isn't wanted.

3. The Achiever: "Vito Corleone" from *The Godfather*, by Mario Puzo

Achievers are often powerful individuals in a story, or are on a steady rise to power. These characters desire success and the recognition that comes with it. Vito Corleone is a classic example of an achiever.

The young Sicilian immigrant comes to America without a cent in his pocket or a single word of English in his vocabulary. From this humble beginning, he ascends to become one of the most powerful men in organized crime.

In a classic line of dialogue, Vito solves a business dispute by making a would-be opponent "an offer he can't refuse." He's willing to go to any lengths to succeed, even if it means killing his enemies.

This doesn't make him a purely evil character. He demonstrates genuine love for his friends and family, and rarely refuses a favor when someone comes to him for help. But he always expects payment for these favors, should he ever ask. And he demands respect from his allies and subordinates.

At one point in the novel, Vito Corleone turns down an offer to become partners in an enterprising drug scheme, which he describes as "a dirty business." Even then, his traits as an Achiever shine through. His avoidance of drugs within his crime syndicate is not purely a moral choice. Vito Corleone managed to acquire owed favors from many politicians during his career, and could persuade them to look the other way in regards to his current illicit operations. However, he fears they will not turn a blind eye to something as extreme as drugs. He makes his choice based on what he feels will be better for business.

His drive for success isn't without consequences. His rise to the top makes him many enemies, and leads to numerous assassination attempts. His life is cut short because of this. His empire is also pulled into a war with the other crime families, and this conflict claims the life of his oldest son, Sonny.

Towards the end of the novel, it seems as if Vito has finally been humbled by his son's death, and has changed his ways. He ends the war and submits to the wishes of the drug enterprise, to protect the lives of his remaining children. But in secret, he lays out a plan to ensure the success of his youngest son and successor, Michael Corleone.

After Vito's death, Michael enacts this plan, which results in the deaths of the heads of the enemy crime families. The crime syndicate that Vito left to his son once again stands above all others.

4. The Romantic: "Dorothy" from *The Wizard of Oz* film, based on the book by L. Frank Baum

Highly emotional characters can be classified as Romantics. Their emotions are what drive their behavior. Dorothy, as depicted in the film adaption, is an example of this personality type.

In the movie, Dorothy is portrayed as a daydreamer who longs for more than the gray world that she lives in. When she arrives in Oz, she is entranced by the wonder and color of everything around her.

Like many Romantics, she sometimes makes rash choices based on her current temperament. When her dog is endangered, she impulsively decides to run away. Soon thereafter, a fortune teller informs Dorothy that her aunt is heart-broken because of her decision. In an instant, Dorothy throws her previous plans to the wind and decides to return home.

Time and again, we witness Dorothy's emotions changing rapidly. In the scene where she meets the cowardly lion, she's at first terrified of the creature. When his aggressive demeanor is revealed to be a hoax, she becomes livid with the animal. Shortly thereafter, she feels empathy for him and invites him to join her on the road to the Emerald city. When he agrees, she's happy to have him along. Her emotions change from fear, to anger, to pity, and to happiness, all within a few minutes. A similar series of emotional swings occur when the great Wizard is revealed to be a hoax.

Romantics are often swept up in the moment. When good things are happening, they are overcome by joy. But when the going gets tough, they tend to lose their cool.

5. The Observer: "Hannibal Lecter," first appearing in *Red Dragon* and later in two sequels and a prequel, by Thomas Harris

The Observer analyzes the world around him in intricate detail, and uses logic and self-reliance to solve his problems. The infamous Dr. Hannibal Lecter fits this personality type perfectly.

Lecter is shown to have an eerily effective ability to read people. During his first encounter with agent Clarice Starling, he detects a subtle accent that she is trying to hide, and notices that some of her articles of clothing are cheaper than others. He quickly determines that she is running from humble beginnings. Based on Clarice trying to hide her accent, as well as her efforts to dress herself up with what little expensive accessories she can afford, he deduces that she's insecure about her past. In many ways, Lecter comes off as an evil Sherlock Holmes—who would be another good example of this personality type.

Lecter does this with many characters throughout the series of novels. He picks up on subtle hints that reveal someone's true nature. He then exploits their shortcomings, bringing other characters to anger, fear, or sadness on a whim.

Like many Observers, he can come across as introverted. When he finds someone to be boring or offensive, he may choose to ignore her completely. He has learned how to withdraw his consciousness into his own thoughts, in a method reminiscent of meditation, so as to shut out the rest of the world.

Hannibal Lecter also displays a great deal of patience and attention to detail in his planning. During his eight years of captivity, he meticulously plans his method of escape. In the books, over a period of several years he acquires the pieces necessary to construct a makeshift handcuff key. Among these pieces are a paperclip and the inside tube of a pen. After eight years of waiting, Lecter secretly masterminds a scenario to create the conditions he needs for success, manipulating his captors into setting things in motion. His plan goes off without a hitch and he escapes captivity.

Once he has escaped, one of his hobbies includes spying on agent Clarice Starling from afar. As his personality type implies, he loves to observe others.

6. The Questioner: "Ian Malcolm" from *Jurassic Park* and its sequel by Michael Crichton

Questioners are hesitant to move forward unless they know that the way is safe. For this reason, a

Questioner's role in a story may range anywhere from the voice of reason to the coward who provides comic relief.

Ian Malcolm from the Jurassic Park novels falls more into the voice of reason category. In these novels, a theme park is being developed which contains live dinosaurs. A scientific breakthrough makes it possible to harvest dinosaur DNA and implant it into the eggs of living creatures. This results in extinct creatures being brought to life in order to populate a zoo the likes of which the world has never seen.

Prior to the park's opening, experts are brought in to observe the park and to give their official yay or nay. One of these individuals is Ian Malcolm, who seems content to say "nay" from the beginning.

Malcolm is troubled by the risks involved. He believes that nature cannot be controlled, and that it will always "find a way." In other words, he doesn't believe that modern technology can keep the dinosaur population in check, or successfully confine them in cages.

He also questions whether humankind has any right to undo natural selection, which "chose" dinosaurs as a species that had to die out. He fears that turning back the clock on evolution could have any number of unforeseen consequences. Because safety is not guaranteed, he does not want the park to move forward.

7. The Adventurer: "Tom Sawyer" and "Huckleberry Finn" from the novels of the same names, by Mark Twain

The Adventurer craves adrenalin and excitement. He wants to experience new things, and doesn't approach danger with the appropriate level of caution.

Both Tom Sawyer and Huckleberry Finn exemplify this type. I decided to select both boys as examples, as their outlooks are very similar (which is why they become such good friends), and they often travel together. Their books follow a similar formula, and are packed with adventures. The boys undergo many dangers, and are even assumed dead by their families at a few points.

The obsessive need for action and adventure becomes prevalent through Tom Sawyer, towards the end of *The Adventures of Huckleberry Finn*. The boys have an African-American friend who is trying to escape slavery, but who has recently been captured and locked in a shed. The boys decide to free him, but Tom insists on making it needlessly complex. Freeing him would be as easy as simply opening the door, but Tom is more interested in the fun of a "daring" escape than an anticlimactic one.

Not all Adventurers will go to such extremes for fun. It should be noted that Tom Sawyer and Huckleberry Finn aren't just Adventurers, but they're also very young Adventurers. Immaturity can shine brightly in this personality type, showcasing a desire to place fun before safety.

8. The Protector: "Gandalf" from *The Hobbit* and *The Lord of the Rings* trilogy by J. R. R. Tolkien

Protectors crave stability and strive to preserve order. Gandalf is a prime example of an effective Protector.

When plans are being formed, Gandalf is often the mastermind who puts everything in order. He then goes to great lengths to ensure that things go according to plan.

Characters that are carefree in nature can irritate Protector types. A case in point is the relationship between Gandalf and two young hobbits, Merry and Pippin. These hobbits being careless individuals, Gandalf often has harsh words for them regarding their foolish antics. But his obsessive need to keep them in line comes from a genuine desire to keep them safe.

He is at even greater odds with the character Denethor, whom he believes to be a derelict leader. Denethor reigns over a kingdom, yet Gandalf feels free—in fact, obliged— to openly chastise him for poor decision making. When Denethor orders his soldiers to flee at the sight of an oncoming enemy, Gandalf usurps his leaderships and commands the troops to prepare for battle.

Gandalf goes to great lengths to protect his friends and allies, and is willing to sacrifice himself for the sake of maintaining order. In many ways, he is a "perfect" Protector: he does not, as a rule, seek greater power, try to impose himself or assume control directly, preferring instead to persuade others to follow his course. When he is compelled by circumstance to take a direct hand, he does so reluctantly—if with little hesitation, knowing that to hesitate may be fatal. Which, for a Protector, is the least acceptable of all outcomes.

9. The Peacemaker: "Peeta" from *The Hunger Games* by Suzanne Collins

Peacemakers desire tranquility and try their best to prevent conflict. These traits are displayed in Peeta, a secondary protagonist from *The Hunger Games*.

Peeta is an excellent example of how one's "script," or Personality Type, can remain consistent in any situation.

The Hunger Games is the story of a fascist society that forces twenty-four children to fight to the death every year as "tributes" for their amusement. Peeta is one of these unlucky few. Even though he's forced into a scenario where he must fight to the death, his qualities as the peacemaker still shine through.

The Games are not an instant fight to the death, but rather a long and drawn out ordeal. During the early days of the games, a number of the wealthier and better trained competitors form an alliance to kill off the bulk of the other children. Peeta, despite coming from a humble background, convinces the "careers," as they are called, to let him into their faction.

His mild-mannered and persuasive nature enables him to talk the others into taking a less violent approach. When the main protagonist has been forced up a tree by the careers, Peeta convinces them to wait her out. In truth, he is stalling for time so that she can escape. Later in the games, he uses camouflage to blend into the environment, so as to stay clear of the violence.

Even when pacifism makes no logical sense, Peeta stays true to his personality type. His tactics focus on avoiding conflict. He cannot prevent the Games from taking lives, but he is compelled to delay the inevitable when it's in his power to do so.

As you start to form a rough sketch of your characters, consider which personality type would fit each character best.

If you're having trouble deciding which personality type fits a character, try the following:

Do an inventory of the character's positive and negative aspects, as you currently envision them. Consider which of these aspects have the greatest impact on the character and her choices, and use those to determine the personality type. Then consider how the character would differ were she assigned a different personality type, to make sure you've chosen the most appropriate one.

There are also many online tests based on the enneagram, which are intended to help people identify their own personality types. You can take these tests from the perspective of your character, but remember to answer each question honestly. Your characters and your novel will suffer if you try to make your hero perfect in every way, or if you try to make your villain "evil" for the sake of being perceived as evil. Answer on behalf of your characters, but as if they were real people.

When determining which personality type fits a character, there's no single right answer. It's even possible for your character to have attributes that aren't easily categorized into one type. In any case, you'll want to experiment with different personality types for each character. This process often requires trial and error.

After all, it's no simple task to comprehend the workings of the mind, and the enneagram is only one way to approach this. But if you make the effort to understand your character's inner workings, you'll build a strong foundation for his other attributes.

Layer 2: The Character in His or Her World

Bartle Types

As discussed earlier, the enneagram alone doesn't define your character. It just offers a basis on which to build. In this section, we're constructing the next layer on top of that foundation: how your characters relate to each other and the world around them.

A character with any given enneagram personality type may or may not be a hero. He may or may not be social. He may or may not be easy to anger. The personality type influences his innermost workings, but it can manifest outwardly in any number of ways.

Bartle Types are different roles that characters take when interacting with the world around them. They're named after Richard Bartle, a British researcher whose 1996 paper formed the basis of this theory. Like the enneagram, Bartle Types can offer insight into who your character is and how he should behave.

The theory of Bartle Types has a fascinating history. Originally, it was used as a means to categorize players in the gaming world. Video gamers (both online and single-player) have a wide variance in play style. This variance is due to the increasing complexity and artistic detail in the games themselves. Video games are no longer focused on completing a singular objective. Rather, many games are now virtual worlds.

This is where Bartle Types connect to writing. They were created in order to classify how people behave within a virtual world, and how they interact with others within that environment.

A gamer's play style remains consistent from one game to another. Even when the game changes, the way that he approaches playing stays the same. Bartle Types are similar to enneagram personality types in this regard. A person doesn't change his unconscious drives from one situation to the next. His approach may vary slightly based on new problems, but his overall approach to overcoming them remains the same.

The four Bartle Types are The Killer, The Achiever, The Explorer, and The Socializer. First, we'll discuss the original definition of these types within the context of video games. Then we'll explore how these types translate to writing characters.

The Killer:

- This is the player who seeks instant gratification, and has an aggressive play style.

- In single-player games, The Killer may forsake the plotline, and instead unleash a violent rampage across the virtual world. He will bring mindless chaos and destruction, and may enjoy causing massive damage in creative ways.

- In multi-player games, it isn't uncommon for The Killer to harass new players and trash talk opponents. His play style is quick and carefree, aiming to destroy as many enemies as possible.

The Achiever:

- This is the player who seeks a challenge from the video game experience.

- In single-player games, Achievers may strive to accomplish every goal within the game. They want to complete the main storyline and gather every collectable item possible.

- In multi-player games, they are very competitive and seek to be the best. Unlike the Killer, they may not attack weak players for instant gratification, but instead seek out enemies who would present a challenge. Their objective is to receive recognition for their superior skills.

The Explorer:

- This player enjoys games from a more in-depth perspective.

- In single-player games, Explorers take their time to really immerse themselves in the plot. They retain more focus than The Killer, who seeks instant gratification, and they take more time to enjoy the artistic appeal of the game than the ever-rushing Achiever.

- Their approach is similar in multi-player games. They want to fully experience the world that the developers created.

The Socializer:

- This player enjoys video games for their interactive appeal.

- Single-player games may not appeal to Socializers.They may, however, enjoy games that offer the ability to form relationships with the non-player characters, based on their choices.

- Socializers are primarily interested in multi-player games. They like games that facilitate interaction with other players. Whether or not they achieve objectives may not matter to them, as long as they are having fun while playing with friends.

So, how do video game play styles translate to fictional characters? Well, observing how people play video games offers insight into human nature, as well as how we function as a society.

When video games went online, it changed everything. For the first time ever, players could interact all over the world, completely *anonymously*. This anonymity freed people to show their true colors.

Every day certain people go to work, and wish that they could curse out their coworkers at the drop of a hat. These same people may secretly desire to smack others around without repercussions. These individuals are freed from the normal social constraints when playing online, and reveal themselves to be Killers.

There are also people who buy expensive clothes or fancy cars, secretly longing for the recognition of others. While they may try to act humble in real life, they may display their vanity more openly online, revealing themselves to be Achievers.

These are just examples, but they illustrate how Bartle Types provide insight into human behavior. They're not just video game play styles. They're windows into how people wish that they could act around one another.

Let's look at the four Bartle Types again. But this time, we'll explore how they may apply to fictional characters.

The Killer

The Killer wants things to be quick and easy. He may not be prone to actual murder, but he may pick a fight if it helps him to get his way.

The Killer doesn't want to waste time, he wants to indulge. If a Killer goes to a bar, seeking a night of "companionship," he won't beat around the bush courting one female all night. Instead, he may approach the first attractive woman that he sees, and make his intentions known outright. If she isn't interested, he shrugs it off and moves to the next target.

In the career world, a Killer may grow tired of a job quickly, and won't hesitate to quit when stress sets in. He seeks a job that isn't stressful, which showcases his natural abilities, so that he can either rise through the ranks quickly, or can effortlessly remain at his current level.

The Killer tends to want things his way, and is not willing to compromise. However, a Killer can be a bit of a wild card when interacting with other Bartle Types.

When amongst other Killers, they will usually get along, provided they don't have conflicting interests. They tend to socialize with individuals who like the same fast-paced activities that they do. They can be brash in nature, so it can work well for them to hang around other Killers, as they tend to have tough skins. But when two Killers have a disagreement, the ensuing conflict can be swift and brutal.

When interacting with Achievers, they may covet their luxuries. Killers tend to lack the time or patience to acquire these things for themselves, and this can lead to contempt. While they may admire each other, as both types can be "cut-throat" in nature, Killers tend to be gung-ho in their endeavors, while Achievers may opt for more careful planning.

When dealing with Explorers, Killers may belittle their artistic and sensitive attributes. As seekers of instant gratification, Killers are unlikely to appreciate the long and tedious projects that appeal to Explorers. Killers enjoy fast paced activities, while Explorers may prefer activities that are slower and can be carefully savored.

With Socializers, Killers can sometimes find companionship. A Killer's "play hard" attitude may compliment a Socializer's carefree outlook. Yet at times, Killers may view Socializers as being clingy, and in need of "tougher skin."

The Achiever

The Achiever pushes hard to reach his goals. He wants to be the best at what he does, and desires the recognition that comes with success.

Unlike Killers, Achievers don't typically move from one mate to another. If they do, it may be in pursuit of an "alpha male" sense of accomplishment. But more frequently, Achievers form an ideal image of the perfect mate. They may go to great lengths to win the affections of a specific companion.

Achievers will strive to succeed in any career, unless they feel that their talents are being wasted. They find pride and prestige in raises, promotions, personal offices, awards, and other perks of success.

Achievers can sometimes be introverted, which can hurt their interactions with the other Bartle Types. However, they are also status conscious, and interaction with others is necessary in order for their accomplishments to be recognized. They desire to be perceived by others as attractive, interesting, and prestigious.

When interacting with Killers, Achievers may be hard pressed to get along nicely. They may disdain a Killer's brash attitude and perceived sloppiness. Still, they are similar in that they both demand to have their own way. This can offer common ground. But it will make matters worse if they have conflicting goals.

When among other Achievers, their interactions vary greatly depending on status. Meeting an Achiever of higher status can result in envy or adoration. Two Achievers of similar status may engage in constant one-upmanship. Meeting an Achiever of lower status can provide a wonderful ego boost, especially if the "lesser" Achiever is willing to listen to a long list of accomplishments.

When faced with Explorers, Achievers may view them as time-wasters. An Explorer may push towards a career in music simply because that is what he loves. Achievers, on the other hand, find it absurd to pursue careers with little chance of success. They may admire Explorers for their drive and tenacity, which is often on a par with that of The Achiever. They may admire, even envy, the Explorer's sheer scope of accomplishment, in contrast to their own, more circumscribed, depth of same. (Compare, for example, an academic with a Ph.D. in one field to someone with multiple lesser degrees in diverse ones.) But the two are usually in pursuit of very different goals.

When interacting with Socializers, the two types tend to get along beautifully. Achievers like to talk about themselves, and Socializers are willing to lend an ear. Seasoned Achievers also tend to throw great parties, which Socializers love to attend. Achievers who come across as arrogant might be off-putting to Socializers. But otherwise, they tend to get along.

The Explorer

The Explorer tends to be creative and artistic. He wants to learn interesting things and revel in new experiences.

In personal relationships, Explorers may be reluctant to settle down. They cherish their independence, as they need the freedom to experience new things. When they do seek out a mate, they will look for someone who appreciates their creative ideas, and won't try to restrain their eccentric tendencies. When they fall in love, it's often profound.

Explorers tend to choose careers that interest them. They are unlikely to stay in a job that is boring and repetitive. They may pursue self-employment or careers that enable them to take creative liberties.

Explorers, like Achievers, can be introverted. This colors their interactions with other Bartle Types.

When dealing with Killers, things can become strained. In high school, for instance, a Killer would be the stereotypical jock, while an Explorer would pursue artistic endeavors. Explorers tend to be sensitive, so the brash behavior of Killers may be hard for them to endure. Both Explorers and Killers enjoy recreational activities, so they may find common ground if their interests don't conflict.

In relation to Achievers, the two types are somewhat removed. Both types may be introverted, but are absorbed in vastly different projects. They have common ground in their desire to succeed, but the goals that they strive for are different. For Explorers, life tends to be about the journey, whereas Achievers keep their eye on the destination.

When Explorers interact with each other, they like to share their insights and creative ideals. Bouncing ideas off of one another can lead to new creative insights. Explorers tend to have more articulated opinions regarding the arts than other Bartle Types, and they enjoy having someone with whom they can discuss arts and culture. In some cases, two Explorers can engage in a competitive conflict, similar to when two Achievers butt heads.

When dealing with Socializers, they tend to get along swimmingly. Explorers often have fascinating things to discuss, and they talk about their projects with a passion that Socializers can appreciate. This can lead to conversations being a bit one-sided, but for the most part, these two types go well together.

The Socializer

The Socializer loves the company of other people. His desire to be around others can lead to a very active lifestyle.

Socializers tend to be naturals when it comes to personal relationships. They're easy to get along with and are great conversationalists. Yet there are exceptions, such as the stereotypical "hopeless romantic."

Socializers excel at jobs that require human interaction. They work well in groups, and have a hard time being isolated in cubicles. "People person" jobs are natural fits for socializers.

Socializers tend to get along with every Bartle Type, as they mingle well in any crowd.

With Killers, they have the most mixed interactions. They are both interested in recreational activities, which can form a common ground. Killers can be crass at times, but Socializers usually aren't easily offended, and tend to be easy-going. For the most part, Socializers are just looking for a good time with friends, and may be wary of the more aggressive Killers, who have a tendency to scare people off.

With Achievers, they tend to get along more consistently. Potential conflicts can come from some Achievers being too vain, but Socializers make an effort to get along with everyone. Achievers love Socializers, as they are willing to hear them boast about their accomplishments. Socializers don't usually mind the boasting if it means being invited to parties or other social gatherings.

With Explorers, Socializers generally interact wonderfully. Explorers are artistic in nature, and Socializers view them as fascinating individuals. Explorers can sometimes be introverted and absorbed in their own projects, but Socializers make enough effort for a connection to be made... often providing the introverted Explorer with a venue she secretly desires.

Socializers tend to thrive among other Socializers. Their common interest in having fun with friends makes their companionship natural. It take a serious conflict for two Socializers to not get along—one which might be realized in games of social "one-upmanship," for instance. But even then, they tend to be forgiving in nature.

As with the enneagram personality types, these generalizations of the Bartle Types are not absolute. Not all Achievers are vain, not all Socializers have countless friends, and not all Killers are ill-tempered. These descriptions may be useful in determining the social interactions of your characters, but they aren't written in stone.

As models for understanding your characters, the enneagram and Bartle Types share some commonalities, but have different concentrations. While the enneagram primarily focuses on the inner workings of your characters, Bartle Types are more about interaction. The enneagram provides answers for *what* and, especially, *why*; Bartle Types answer *how*: how they interact with their environment, and how they interact with others. While there will be some overlap, a character's enneagram personality type need not be congruent with his Bartle type. Humans are complex and conflicted beings, and it's not uncommon for a person's inner drives and motivations to be contradicted by his external actions.

As we did with the enneagram, let's apply the Bartle Types to some well-known fictional characters. Since the Bartle Types are about how characters interact with their worlds, we'll use characters from the same stories. We'll analyze one set of characters from the Harry Potter series, and another from the Hunger Games.

As before, it must be stressed that this list is not official. This is my own analysis, intended to provide a more concrete picture of the Bartle Types and how they may operate in fiction.

Harry Potter

The Killer: Malfoy

While Voldemort would be the obvious example, I want to stress that not all "Killers" must be actual murderers.

Time and again, Draco Malfoy demonstrates that he must have things his way. Being from a noble background, he's also used to having things handed to him. In the second novel, Malfoy becomes the "seeker" of the Slytherin quidditch team. Other characters suspect that this is due to Malfoy's father equipping the team with new broomsticks. Yet Malfoy isn't bothered that he was handed the position without earning it.

Malfoy tends to be very abrasive in nature. He says what's on his mind at all times, even when it's downright cruel. He feels that others should submit to him, and uses his father's influence to bend the school to his whims.

His crass actions tend to put him at odds with the protagonists. Most of his allies are those that have either been bought or intimidated into loyalty.

The Achiever: Hermione

From her earliest introduction, Hermione is shown to be assertive and driven. Before classes have even started, she's already mastered a number of basic spells and read her textbooks.

She takes her studies very seriously. She's usually the one who comes up with plans, and shows disdain when other characters are careless. This colors her interactions with her friends, especially early in the series.

At times, her attitude can come across as arrogant or condescending. Early in the first school year, she berates Ron for poorly executing a spell, and then revels in praise as she casts the spell correctly.

Hermione is so driven to be the best that she is willing to go to extremes. In one of the novels, she even violates wizarding laws by manipulating time. She does this so that she can attend multiple classes simultaneously, and excel faster than she could have otherwise.

The Explorer: Luna

We see traits of The Explorer in the quiet and interesting Luna. She is portrayed as a bit of a social outcast. Other characters perceive her as "weird," even in a world full of wizards, magic and monsters.

She's shown to have an interest in artistic pursuits, and enjoys new experiences. She's aware of mystical creatures that even other wizards don't know about. One such example includes tiny unseen creatures that float around people's heads and muddy their thoughts. Her methods of detecting and warding off these creatures are "creative" to say the least.

The Socializer: Harry

Having been confined to a tiny closet for years, Harry is very enthusiastic to finally make some friends.

While still socially awkward at times, Harry shows a genuine desire to get along with others and form new relationships. His charismatic skills improve as the series progresses, as is evident when a group of students declaring themselves "Dumbledore's Army" look to him for leadership.

When Harry looks forward to going back to school, he doesn't seem eager to learn new magic as much as he's eager to reunite with friends.

Throughout the series, Harry forms many loyal companions through his likeable personality and genuine presence.

The Hunger Games

The Killer: Cato

Cato establishes himself as the head of the deadly "careers" through sheer power and force.

Like the other careers, he comes from a background of far better means and training than the protagonists, and actually volunteered for the Hunger Games because he wanted to be in them.

He's portrayed as being extremely impatient and constantly wanting things his way. He even goes to the extreme of killing another career in his alliance for failing to protect the supplies while he was away.

The Achiever: Katniss

Katniss didn't hone her abilities through intensive training or expensive equipment. Instead, she developed her skills through necessity, so as to be self-reliant and provide food for her mother and sister.

When Katniss volunteers to take her little sister's place in the Hunger Games, she makes her a promise. She assures her sister that she'll try to win.

While her objective is to win, she takes a different approach than the careers, who are almost all Killers. She plays the game for the long haul, wanting to ride things out to the end smoothly and carefully.

At the start of the games, there's a bloodbath as the Killer types fight over a surplus of supplies in the center of the arena. Katniss doesn't take part in this brawl, or in any other early conflict that she can avoid.

Playing it smart, she secretly makes camp in high trees. She uses her wits in other ways as well, such as sabotaging the supplies of the careers, and contemplating the possibility of tricking the careers into eating poisoned berries.

The Explorer: Rue

Rue is an Explorer even in the literal sense of the word.

She's a tiny girl with no combat experience. In order to survive, she has to be more creative than those who are hunting her.

She is revealed to have an exceptional ability to climb trees. Even Katniss, who uses trees for safety, doesn't do so in a manner as impressive as Rue. Due to her light weight and agility, she can actually climb trees to their peaks, as the lighter branches are able to support her tiny frame. She can move silently from one tree to another, allowing her to go to and fro throughout the entire arena undetected.

She's also shown to have exceptional observational skills and some creativity. When Katniss is trapped in a tree with careers waiting for her below, it's Rue who shows her a hive of poisonous insects hanging from a branch. Katniss uses Rue's plan and it saves her life.

The Socializer: Peeta

Even before the games begin, Peeta is shown to be a likeable character. When Katniss is told that her attitude won't win her sponsors, she is advised to look at Peeta, who seems to have the right approach. The citizens of Panem are instantly drawn to his charming personality.

When the competition begins, Peeta convinces the careers not to kill him and joins them briefly, though only to protect Katniss.

He comes off as being a bit shy, but this doesn't prevent him from being a Socializer and winning people over to his side. Eventually, he even wins the love of Katniss.

For writers, Bartle Types are a useful tool for defining how your characters interact with each other and their societies. When selecting a type for your character, it's helpful to look at the character's situation at the start of your story, and to ask the following:

- How did he arrive in these circumstances?

- What decisions led to his current social status?

Your answers to these questions will help you to identify the most fitting Bartle Type for that character.

The Five Great Relationships

How your characters interact within their worlds is also determined by their social identities.

Throughout an individual's life, certain relationships help mold who he is. A character's social identity determines his responsibilities, as well as his social status.

There's a theory of social identity that dates back over two thousand years, and is attributed to the Chinese philosopher Confucius (551-479 BC). He taught that there are five main relationships in our lives that shape us as people. These relationships are:

1. Ruler and Subject

2. Parents and Child

3. Husband and Wife

4. Elder Sibling and Younger Sibling

5. Friend and Friend

It should be noted that the natures of some of these relationships have evolved since the time of Confucius. When Confucius first created this system, it classified the responsibilities of an individual into simple white and black rankings, in which certain individuals always rank higher than others. This was in order to teach people the responsibilities that were expected of them by society. They were to show respect and adherence to those above them, and show responsibility and benevolence to those below them.

For instance, the third relationship, "Husband and Wife," dictated that the husband was above the wife in the social order. As such, he was expected to care for her well-being, and she in turn was to show him adherence. Obviously, one gender having automatic authority over another is an outmoded worldview.

But the five relationships *are* still relevant. While husbands and wives do not "outrank" one another, having a husband or a wife *does* affect your responsibilities.

In this chapter, we'll discuss how these relationships can help form your characters. Knowing your characters' formative relationships will give you greater insight into who they are in society.

Even if your hero's parents will never be mentioned in your book, it's still helpful for *you* to know who they are, and how they helped shape your character into who he is today.

Let's go over each relationship in detail and explore how they are important:

1. Ruler and Subject (Government)

Your character's relationship to his government is an important one. Consider your character's political views. Is he living in accord with his government, or is he at odds with it?

A novel's political climate is sometimes used to set the plot in motion. Perhaps the government is inept and crime runs rampant: thus the need for a hero to arise. Or perhaps the government is *too* ruthless at crime and punishment, and has become tyrannical. Your hero might even be on perfectly pleasant terms with his government, and seeks to help them in their endeavors.

The relationship between Ruler and Subject also creates a fertile breeding ground for villains. Sometimes the corrupt Ruler is the villain, or sometimes the villain is a disillusioned Subject who incorrectly believes that the Ruler must be stopped. It is also a potential spawning ground for the antihero: one whose "villainous" actions spring from rebellion against authority... even if there's good reason for rebellion.

2. Parents and Child

Your characters' upbringings will play a large role in who they are as adults. As mentioned earlier, it's important for *you* to have this information even if it's never shared with the reader. Knowing where your characters comes from can help you to better understand where they are today.

Consider that your hero and villain may be who they are because of how they were treated as children.

And if your character *is* a parent, then you have to consider the responsibilities that are expected of him. Having a dependant will impact every decision that he makes.

3. Husband and Wife (Romance)

When you marry someone, or even become romantically involved with another person, it changes your life in a profound way.

You now have someone to consult before making huge decisions, and someone whose well-being you must consider before making choices on your own.

Your character may be hesitant to march headlong into danger if someone is waiting for him at home. And sometimes a significant other can greatly influences one's decisions, as seen in Macbeth.

4. Elder Sibling and Younger Sibling

Siblings can play a vital role in how your character grew up. There's evidence to suggest personality differences between people who were raised as an only child, those who were raised around siblings of the opposite gender, those who were raised around siblings of the same gender, those who were the eldest child, those who were the youngest child, and those who were born in the middle.

Consider whether or not your character has siblings, even if they don't appear in your novel. Ask yourself how your character's childhood was affected by his siblings.

In a character's adult life, siblings may continue to play a significant role. Older siblings may never stop looking out for their younger siblings, and could become overly protective of other people who aren't family members. The "baby" of the family may have an unconscious expectation of always getting his own way, even in his adult life.

5. Friend and Friend

Your character's friends and allies will be an important part of his life.

How many friends does your character have? Do any stand out? How loyal and trustworthy are they? How does your character treat them in return?

These are all questions that must be asked when developing your character. There are times in our own lives when we depend greatly on our friends for support. Why would this be different for your character?

Having a healthy, or failing relationship with one's friends can greatly impact your character's immediate future.

Now that we're familiar with the five relationships, let's examine a few well known fictional characters, and see how these relationships helped to shape them.

Katniss, from *The Hunger Games* by Suzanne Collins

Katniss is a prime example of how these relationships can dictate a character's responsibilities. A lot of weight is placed on her shoulders.

The relationship between Katniss and her Government is an unpleasant one. In *The Hunger Games*, the government is tyrannical. They have divided society into a number of districts, separating wealthy communities from poor ones.

Every year, each district must offer up two children to fight to the death in a tournament, and Katniss becomes one of these victims.

Her involvement in the Games is due to another relationship: Siblings. Katniss' younger sister was first chosen to be one of the competitors, but Katniss volunteered to take her place.

This wasn't the first time that Katniss had to look out for her younger sister, due to another relationship: Parent and Child. Katniss' mother is a troubled, depressed person, and this has caused Katniss to mature at a faster rate than most girls. The household has depended on her for years to provide food.

During her time in the tournament, the Friend relationship helps to guide her actions. She takes a protective role over her friend Rue, and later her friend Peeta. Her relationship with Peeta later evolves into a Romance relationship.

Bruce Wayne, from the extensive *Batman* franchise; original concept by Bob Kane and Bill Finger

This character (better known under his super hero alias, Batman) has appeared in almost every form of media imaginable. He's been in comic books, graphic novels, basic novels, movies, television, and more. His history has undergone innumerable changes and revisions since 1939. But many of his defining characteristics and the relationships that formed them have remained consistent throughout.

Bruce has a varied relationship with Government. Gotham city is often portrayed as having a failing legal system and corrupt public officials. The streets are unsafe, thus Bruce Wayne's need to don his costume and fight crime. On the other hand, he's on good terms with some public officials, such as Police Commissioner Gordon. This relationship gives Bruce a foot in the door for his freelance crime fighting, and is generally sufficient to forestall zealous police pursuit of his vigilantism.

In terms of Sibling relationships, Bruce has none—and his character manifests stereotype features of only children. He is highly motivated, driven to succeed, to be perfect: his youthful model for "competition" was not siblings, but rather his father... who he sometimes still compares himself unfavorably to, even as an adult. He is "spoiled" not merely in the sense of being born into privilege, but also in the sense of always expecting to get his way. Indeed, it is just such an instance that leads to the great tragedy of his life.

Bruce has a unique relationship with his Parents. He witnessed them being murdered at a young age, and this tragic event is what drives his crusade for safety and justice. In his adult life, he still remembers lessons that his father taught him. Additionally, he has an ongoing "father" figure in Alfred... albeit one whose advice he ignores as often as heeds. Furthermore, he himself acts as a "parent" to a succession of youngsters—legally as well as figuratively, in that as Bruce Wayne he adopted all the boys who became Batman's crime fighting partner, Robin, over the years.

The Friend and Romance relationships also play a large role in Bruce's life. In order to protect those he associates with in his civilian guise, he keeps his identity a secret from his enemies. Maintaining dual identities has a dual edge, however: as Bruce Wayne, he can only get so close to others, without endangering the secret he preserves to protect them. This often causes failure in relationships he might wish to advance, but cannot see ways through to doing so.

Will Graham, from *Red Dragon* by Thomas Harris

In the novel *Red Dragon*, Will Graham is a retired criminal profiler who is asked to return to the FBI. There's a serial killer on the loose who has been stumping the police, and the last two killers of this caliber were captured by Graham.

Will Graham is on decent terms with his Government. He was formerly an agent enforcing the government's laws.

He is torn between his sense of duty to the public and his sense of duty to his family. Will now has a wife (Romance) and step-son (Parent and Child). They are both concerned for his well-being, and their concern makes him hesitant to take the case. He eventually does, begrudgingly, and thinks about his family often.

The Friend relationship could be loosely applied to the relationship between Will Graham and Hannibal Lecter. Hannibal is one of the serial killers that Will caught in the past. Hannibal feels some level of respect for Will for having caught him, but this emotion is more or less one-sided.

Will goes to Lecter for help on the new case, because he feels the best way to catch this new killer is to think like a killer. And who better to ask how a killer thinks than a convicted serial murderer? During this new case he forms a connection with Hannibal that he had hoped to avoid.

Will's interactions with Hannibal prove to be interesting, and end up influencing the progression of the case. Sometimes for better, and sometimes for worse.

Fredo Corleone, from *The Godfather* by Mario Puzo

This character plays a minor role in the novel and film of the same name, but his character is expanded upon in the second film (of which there was no novel).

Like all members of the Corleone crime family, Fredo has a strained relationship with his Government. But I chose him for this list primarily because of his relationships with Siblings.

Fredo is viewed by others, including his family members, as being weak and inept. This is partially due to an unfair curve—his family being made up of many great minds and fierce hearts.

There are four siblings in Fredo's life: his brothers Sonny and Michael, his sister Connie, and his adopted brother Tom Hagen. His role within the novel is due to his relationship with Sonny and Michael.

Sonny is Fredo's elder brother, and is an extremely fearsome fighter. Michael is Fredo's younger brother, and proves to be the most cunning of his siblings. Fredo appears to be dumb and weak in comparison to them.

When their father, Vito Corleone, is hospitalized, Sonny is the natural successor who takes control of the family. But Fredo reveals later that he was unhappy about this.

Much later, Vito and Sonny have both passed on, Vito due to failing health and Sonny having been gunned down. Much to Fredo's dismay, he is passed over entirely and Michael is chosen to become the new leader.

This leads to Fredo unwittingly betraying the family in the second film. He suffers from an inferiority complex and has a need to prove himself. He resents that his younger brother "looks after" him. His struggling relationship with his brother leads to poor and rash decisions on his part.

Alexander DeLarge, from *A Clockwork Orange* by Anthony Burgess

Alex is a young and troublesome man in the somewhat disturbing tale of *A Clockwork Orange*.

He has an indifferent relationship to his Government, engaging in a number of sinister crimes for a pastime. The Government of Alex's world is portrayed as somewhat inept. Crime runs rampant in the streets and jails are overcrowded. He views his truancy officer with disrespect and when arrested is hostile towards the police.

His relationship with his Government takes a sharp turn for the worse when he's selected as a test subject for a new rehabilitation experiment. The Government then plays a role in Alex's life that is beyond measure, as the experiment attempts to change Alex's ways by annihilating his free will.

Alex's Parent and Child relationship is an unhealthy one. His parents seem to be somewhat afraid of him. In the novel, it's implied that he used physical force at some time or another to gain adherence from his parents. While they're unaware of his criminal activities, they ignore his oddities around the home, such as staying out late, playing music loudly late at night, and missing school for days at a time.

Friend and Friend plays a big role in Alex's life early in the story. He commands a small gang of subordinates who he often mistreats. His aggressive behavior towards them grants him the position of leader within the group, but this later leads to the others betraying him. Alex's friend's scheme against him, and their betrayal leads to him being captured by the police.

Alex is the only character on my list that doesn't have a single healthy relationship within *any* of the five. This leads to his downfall and capture, and crushing isolation when he is released from prison. It's not until the end of the novel that he forms a shaky but somewhat positive relationship with the Government, this being due to the rehabilitation procedure used on Alex becoming controversial. Alex is offered bribes for siding with the Government in the ensuing media frenzy, thus creating a flimsy alliance.

In the very last chapter (which was originally omitted in the American version of the book and wasn't included in the film adaptation), Alex starts to feel remorse for his current way of life. The book ends with him having a desire to pursue the Romance and Parent and Child relationships, and hoping that if he does have a son someday, that his child won't turn out like him.

When determining your character's relationships, consider what you want him to experience during the course of your story. A character's relationships can limit what is possible, at least within the bounds of believability. For example, a fugitive who's being hunted by his government can't easily walk into a courthouse and apply for a marriage license. A person with a large family dependent on his support is unlikely to wander off on adventures at the drop of a hat.

Conversely, relationships can also open new possibilities, and may prove to be rich sources of conflict. Governments tend to favor their more "important" (wealthy, well-connected) subjects, intervening in their affairs whether asked to or not... occasionally even when asked *not* to, if the government or one of its organs sees its interests to be otherwise. Large extended families can carry on vendettas for years, even generations. People with many friends can call on their help—in some cases, their friends may become offended if they *aren't* asked to help out. Keep these factors in mind as you work through the five great relationships.

Layer 3: The Character in Your Story

Archetypes

In the last two layers, we developed your characters as people. In this layer, we'll develop your characters as characters. In other words, we'll consider the roles that they play in the structure of your story.

Similar character roles appear across all, or nearly all, cultures and religions, permeating folk and mythic traditions. They are immediately recognizable to readers from any other culture. We've seen characters like The Hero and The Mentor time and again, and the reason writers keep using them is because we know who they are. These are the Archetypes.

As defined by Carl Jung, archetypes are recurring themes that result from "countless experiences of our ancestors. They are, as it were, the psychic residue of numberless experiences of the same type." According to Jung, they are not merely familiar to us from having encountered them through our own culture's traditions: they are rooted in the collective unconscious of all human beings.

Careful use of archetypes can let you tap into the unconscious mind of your reader. Every hero that they've ever encountered is stored within the unconscious mind. When your hero steps into the spotlight, your reader instantly knows that this is the person they're supposed to empathize with and cheer for.

This is true for all archetypes. They are recognized roles that your characters can step into. When an archetype is used effectively in your writing, it has the effect of triggering emotions from deep within your reader.

Here are eight well-known and frequently used archetypes:

Hero

This is the central character of your novel. The story is typically told from the perspective of the Hero, and we are meant to empathize with his journey.

At the beginning of the novel, the Hero is typically portrayed as an "everyman," an ordinary individual. This is to make it easier for the reader to relate to the character, so that they'll want to walk in his shoes.

Starting with the Hero as an everyman also leaves room for him to grow and progress throughout his journey. The Hero has much to experience before he's ready to face his final challenge. He has to improve his skills, gain knowledge, and overcome inner demons in order to move forward.

How interesting would the Harry Potter series be if Harry was already an expert wizard when we first met him? It would be harder to establish common ground with him, and his struggle against Voldemort would seem less harrowing.

Heroes are not usually portrayed as perfect. This would also make them less relatable, and having a hero with no imperfections would dampen the suspense. Give your Hero some vices, and perhaps let him overcome a few of the worst ones as the story progresses.

The Hero typically prevails by the end of the novel, even if victory costs him his life.

Shadow

The Shadow often represents the darkness within the Hero, a reflection of what the Hero would become if he turned to evil. This character's morals are tarnished, and he's naturally at odds with the Hero. Sometimes the Shadow and the Hero share a connection, such as a familial bond or shared history.

Typically, this archetype is used for the main antagonist of your novel. However, secondary villains and other characters can also play this role. One example would be a friend of the Hero who has malice in his heart, and eventually turns evil; but this example can also be attached to the Shapeshifter.

A Shadow character is usually dark, menacing and dangerous. He must be a real threat to the hero. This is especially true if you want the Shadow to be the main villain. Readers must be unsure that the Hero will be triumphant. To establish this uncertainty, the Hero' nemesis must be powerful.

Mentor

The Mentor is a wise character who assists the Hero on his path. He helps the Hero rise from an everyman to a champion.

A mentor character can serve as a useful storytelling device. He may challenge the Hero to reach new levels of knowledge and skill, making it possible for the Hero to move forward in the story. The Mentor will sometimes bestow gifts upon the Hero, such as magic or powerful items to aid in his journey.

Mentors are typically portrayed as elderly, to convey the sense that they're carriers of wisdom. This triggers immediate recognition of the archetype, since we typically associate wisdom with age.

Also, it's common for mentors to leave the Hero at some point in the story, forcing him to take what he's learned and apply it on his own.

Herald

This character brings news and information to the Hero.

The Herald may be a messenger, a prophet, a doomsayer, or so on. The Herald is usually the character who calls the Hero to undertake his journey. A Herald may also inform him when there is a dramatic turn of events, or change in the world.

Threshold Guardian

Your Hero will endure many tests during his journey. Some of these tests may be embodied as Threshold Guardians.

A Threshold Guardian is a character who serves as an obstacle between the Hero and the next stage of his quest. The motivations of Threshold Guardians can be varied. They may have been sent by the villain to slow the Hero's progress, or perhaps they are acting independently. But their role within your story is consistent: they are a challenge that the Hero must overcome, making the hero stronger in the process.

Shapeshifter

The Shapeshifter is a character who undergoes a dramatic change in the story. It may be a physical change, or a change of allegiance. Shapeshifters are often used to bring about a sudden twist or a looming uncertainty in a novel.

Shapeshifters are not usually literal shapeshifters, although they can be. The term refers to their potential to change midway through the story.

A character who suddenly betrays the Hero would be a Shapeshifter, as would an enemy who becomes an unexpected ally. In some cases, the Shapeshifter is merely a character who personifies a desire to change, and the archetype would apply to him regardless of whether or not he actually does change during the course of the story.

The twists and betrayals that this character offers can make your novel less predictable.

Trickster

The Trickster is a cunning and sometimes humorous character who seeks to upset the status quo. He brings chaos into the Hero's world, and often changes it in some significant way. A Trickster may also serve as comic relief within a story, or can be a villain in his own right.

The motivations for Tricksters to overturn the norm may vary. In some cases they simply seek amusement. But they may also have darker intentions, such as convincing the hero that his journey is pointless.

Ally

Allies are characters who help the hero to overcome obstacles on his journey. These are the characters who stand beside him and help him to achieve his goals. In some cases, the hero's love interest would fall into the archetype of Ally.

There are more archetypes beyond these eight, but these are the most common, and understanding them will be enough to get you started. It's also important to note that you won't always use all eight of these archetypes in your work. Many stories only contain a few archetypal characters.

Also, some characters may fill more than one archetypal role within a story. As explained by Christopher Vogler in *The Writer's Journey*:

> The archetypes can be thought of as masks, worn by the characters temporarily as they are needed to advance the story. A character may enter the story performing the function of a herald, then switch masks to function as a trickster, a mentor, and a shadow.

In order to show how the archetypes play off of each other, we'll look at sets of examples that come from the same stories. However, many modern novels don't use all eight archetypes as they are classically defined. That being said, I selected stories that come close, and filled all eight spots as accurately as I could.

I must give my little disclaimer again, but this time it's only partially true. *Some* of these archetype examples are official. For instance, in most works of fiction the character who fills the role of The Hero is no secret. But I want to offer examples of all eight archetypes, so I'm including my own unofficial analysis.

Here are examples of each archetype from novels and cinema:

Harry Potter series, by J.K. Rowling

Hero: Harry Potter

Harry Potter exemplifies the classic Hero archetype. He's introduced to us as a humble "nobody," who is mistreated and ignored.

Suddenly, Harry's world changes. He learns that he's a wizard, and that there's a dark force that seeks to kill him.

This leads to many adventures. Harry gains Allies, fights Threshold Guardians, and increases his knowledge and skill level along the way.

His many trials are building up to an epic battle that must occur between himself and the Shadow.

Shadow: Voldemort

Voldemort is a classic embodiment of this archetype. He is, very literally, a dark and menacing figure. He's cloaked in black and has snake-like facial features.

He also represents the darkest aspects of the wizarding world, such as lust for power, and a genocidal intolerance of wizards who are not "pure bloods."

Voldemort personifies evil and is bent on destroying the Hero. Like many Shadows, he shares a connection with the Hero—in this case it's a literal psychic connection. He's one of the most popular Shadows in modern fiction.

Mentor: Albus Dumbledore

Again, we see a very classic use of an archetype with Dumbledore as the Mentor.

He's elderly and wise. He cares for Harry's safety, but knows that in the end Harry will have to face the evil alone. For this reason he does what he can to prepare Harry, but doesn't like to fight battles for him.

Harry Potter has many teachers at his school, but it is Dumbledore who bestows knowledge on Harry when he needs it the most.

Herald: Rubeus Hagrid

Within Harry's story there are many characters who come with important news, but Hagrid is arguably the most important.

It is Hagrid who informs Harry that he is a wizard. Hagrid is also the one who physically escorts Harry from his day to day world into the world of wizarding.

Hagrid further explains to Harry (and the reader) the details of Harry's hidden past, as well as the looming threats to come. Hagrid is also the character who first introduces the Hero to the dreaded name of Voldemort.

Hagrid's initial appearance changes Harry's life dramatically, and sets the Hero's journey in motion.

Threshold Guardian: Severus Snape

Threshold Guardians are usually unconvinced of the Hero's abilities or special nature. This remains true for Severus Snape.

As Harry strives to do what's right, this often puts him at odds with the rules of the school—the rules that Snape strives to enforce. He has little tolerance for troublemakers, and is often glaring at Harry and his Allies.

At first, Severus serves as a more passive Threshold Guardian. He doubts Harry's power, and is not above being snide towards him. But rarely does Snape stand as a physical force that must be overcome.

This changes as the series progresses. Eventually, it's revealed that Voldemort has the power to read Harry's thoughts. In order to protect himself, Harry must endure intense training under Snape. Snape uses aggressive and even painful mindreading spells on Harry, which Harry must overcome if he's to stand a chance against Voldemort.

Snape serves as a Threshold Guardian following the death of Dumbledore, when he seizes control of the school. He has to be defeated so that the school can mobilize against the forces of evil.

In the end, Snape is revealed to not be evil. This is often the case with Threshold Guardians. They hinder the Hero at first, but their challenge proves to be beneficial. Threshold Guardians are not required to be bad guys.

Shapeshifter: Draco Malfoy

Draco's intentions are unclear from the start. When something goes wrong at Hogwarts, Harry and his friends often look at Draco as their first suspect, but learn that he isn't the culprit. During the early years at Hogwarts, Draco is little more than a troublemaker or a watered down version of a Threshold Guardian.

In later years, however, his darker tendencies come to the forefront. Draco shifts from being a cowardly bully to a spiteful enemy. He operates as an undercover minion for Voldemort. He orchestrates dark happenings within the school, the worst being the teleportation of Voldemort's followers into Hogwarts.

When it appears certain that Draco is truly evil, the character undergoes another shift. When ordered, he's hesitant and ultimately unable to kill Dumbledore.

Later, we learn that his heart isn't with Voldemort and the dark wizards. His own allegiance is uncertain.

At the story's conclusion, Draco is shown to be on friendly terms with Harry. Draco's changes in alignment and the uncertainty of his intentions make him an excellent example of a Shapeshifter.

Trickster: Fred and George Weasley

Fred and George, or simply "the Weasley twins" are tricksters in every sense.

These brothers revel in upsetting the blowhards and breaking all the rules. They often belittle other characters (primarily their little brother Ron) in a teasing fashion, as Tricksters often do.

When Dumbledore's role as headmaster is usurped by a woman who imposes many unjust rules on the school, it's these two who raise a bit of anarchy to lift everyone's spirits.

Ally: Ron Weasley and Hermione Granger

Harry has many Allies during his journeys, but none are as important as Ron and Hermione.

They become close friends with Harry during his first year at Hogwarts. While the trio sometimes squabble amongst themselves, they always overcome these disagreements and continue their friendship.

Ron and Hermione prove to be invaluable Allies during Harry's many encounters with dark forces. They are brave when necessary, and have unique talents that they bring to the table.

The Godfather, by Mario Puzo

Hero: Michael Corleone

Michael is introduced as what his mafia family members call "a civilian," an individual on the right side of the law. He's not part of his father's criminal empire, and has no desire to be. But events beyond his control force his hand, and he's compelled to defend his family from a dire threat.

This is a classic setup for the Hero: an "everyman" who is forced into action. This allows us to identify Michael as the story's central character, despite the story's point of view jumping between various characters.

Throughout the novel, Michael must face many hardships. He overcomes these trials and by the end of the novel, he becomes the head of the Corleone crime family.

Of course, some may find it a stretch to consider a mafia boss a "hero." Heroes don't always have to be good guys: this is why "antiheroes" are still heroes.

Regardless of activities or virtues, they still fit the archetype.

Shadow: Virgil Sollozzo

The main antagonist of The Godfather is usually considered to be Emilio Barzini. But Emilio plays his hand in the background, mostly unseen to the reader.

Virgil, on the other hand, is given more face time with the characters, and embodies the Shadow in the classic sense. He's dark and menacing, with dangerous intentions. This is an example of how the Shadow it not necessarily the major villain, although he often is.

Sollozzo is shown to be immoral even among criminals. He seeks to establish a drug empire in America, and develops a vendetta against the Corleone family when they refuse to help him. He attempts to have Vito Corleone assassinated on two occasions, in hopes that his successor, Sonny, will be more willing to make a deal with him.

Virgil is killed halfway through the story, but his actions continue to drive the plot, as his blood war carries on until the novel's end draws near.

Mentor: Vito Corleone

Vito is Michael's father. He shares a similar desire with Michael, in that Vito doesn't want his son to live a life of crime.

Vito's role as the Mentor is a bit different from most. Many Mentors assume their roles early on, teaching the Hero from an early point in the story. But throughout most of the novel Michael is left to make decisions on his own, or with the help of lesser Mentors. It isn't until late in the novel that Michael begins to flourish under his father's wing. Vito grooms Michael as a successor, and gives him advice that saves his life.

Herald: Tom Hagen

Tom Hagen is a personal advisor within the Corleone crime family. He is also often used as a negotiator and messenger.

His role as the Herald isn't the classic depiction, as he's not the character who starts Michael on his journey, although he does play a part.

More often, Hagen functions as a Herald to other characters. He delivers a message from Sollozzo to Sonny, saying that Sollozzo wants a truce. He's sent to clarify matters with a film producer who's at odds with Vito's godchild. And he's the one who reveals Sonny's death to his father, Vito.

Tom relays pieces of news throughout the story, and they are often ill-tidings. In the film sequel, Tom plays a more direct Herald and delivers bad news directly to Michael, such as the loss of his unborn child.

Threshold Guardian: Sonny Corleone

Vito is hospitalized when Michael decides to join the family business, and it's Sonny who voices his disapproval of Michael's sudden change of heart.

Sonny isn't a typical Threshold Guardian in that he doesn't have to be defeated by Michael in order for progress to be made. But Sonny is a different type of Threshold Guardian in that Michael must convince Sonny of his worth before he'll let Michael in.

After the attempt on their father's life, Michael comes to the family compound and asks how he can help. Sonny refuses to give Michael a job beyond minding the phones.

Later, Michael volunteers to be the one to kill Sollozzo. Sonny originally ridicules him, deriding him as a "nice college boy." Sonny is currently acting as the boss, and Michael cannot attempt to avenge his father without Sonny's approval.

Eventually, Sonny is persuaded and Michael proves himself worthy of this trust.

Shapeshifter: Salvatore Tessio

Tessio is an example of a Shapeshifter whose disloyalty is unknown until it's revealed as a sudden plot twist.

After the death of Vito, Michael assumes control of the family. Vito warned him in advance that the other families might try to kill him as soon as he ascended to power. The most likely tactic would be to use someone close to Michael, and this person would offer a peace meeting—at which Michael would be killed.

As Vito predicted, Salvatore Tessio comes to Michael and promises to arrange a meeting with the Barzini family. A long and trusted ally of Vito, Tessio proves to be the traitor.

It's inferred that Tessio didn't approve of Michael's rise to leadership. Being Michael's elder, he was jealous of being passed over for promotion.

Be sure to give your Shapeshifter a motivation for his sudden change, as Mario Puzo did. Resist the urge to throw in unrealistic twists just for the sake of having them.

Trickster: Jules Segal

This character didn't appear in the film, but is in the novel. He's a doctor who is introduced later in the book, who seeks to upset the status quo.

He has very liberal opinions, particularly in regards to social norms and sexuality. He's not above outright insulting society for having what he regards as backwards views. He also exhibits arrogance towards characters who disagree with him.

He seeks to change how people see the world, but not for the sake of chaos like some tricksters. Instead, he hopes to enlighten those around him, which is another possible motivation for Tricksters.

Ally: Peter Clemenza

Michael had many Allies, many of which fit other archetypes. Peter Clemenza proves himself to be a valuable ally to Michael, as he was to Vito. He carries out missions without question, and is shown to be one of the most loyal members of the Corleone crime family.

The Hobbit, by J. R. R. Tolkien

Hero: Bilbo Baggins

As with many Heroes, we are introduced to Bilbo as an ordinary, seemingly unremarkable individual. He even seems a bit cowardly, and it takes a great deal of encouragement for him to undertake the journey.

Bilbo comes from a community that cherishes peace and quiet. Those who disturb the calm with adventures are ill thought of. Despite this, Bilbo eventually leaves his comfortable home in search of treasure.

Initially, he is naive in dealing with the greater world outside of his community. But he endures many hardships during his travels, and this makes him grow tougher over time. Eventually, his traveling companions begin looking to him for help on a regular basis.

At the story's conclusion, he returns home from his adventure with many treasures. He shares his newfound wealth with his family and community.

Shadow: The Goblins

For this book, I chose a collective presence as the Shadow.

The Goblins are the most constant threat to Bilbo during his journey. They attack him at several points during the novel, and seem to represent all that is evil in the world. They are greedy, hateful, and love to hurt others. In most respects they are the mirror opposite of the civility and comfort that Bilbo prizes.

The Goblins are monsters both in personality and appearance, and are ghastly creatures. One of their more dastardly actions includes killing and eating the ponies of Bilbo and his traveling companions.

In the end, the Goblins provide the focus that rallies all the "good" forces of the world to set aside their own rivalries and act together. No matter their differences, they all know evil when they see it.

Mentor and Herald: Gandalf

Gandalf plays such an important part in this book that he encompassed two archetypes. He serves as both the Mentor and the Herald.

When Bilbo is sitting peacefully on his porch, it's Gandalf who comes to his house and talks of grand adventures. He acts as the Herald, as he's the one who gets Bilbo to leave his home and start his quest. His role as the Herald continues throughout the book, constantly vanishing and reappearing within the traveling party and informing them of some upcoming threat.

He also acts as the Mentor as he dispenses more wisdom than any other character in the book. He plans most of the journey, and is shown to be wise. And like most mentors, he's in his later years.

Threshold Guardian: Smaug

Bilbo must face a dastardly Threshold Guardian. While some Threshold Guardians are not villains, Smaug is evil in every way.

This dragon stands as the greatest obstacle between Bilbo, the dwarves, and their treasure. Smaug guards his hoard fiercely, and is infuriated when a single cup is taken from his loot.

While Bilbo is not the one who physically defeats Smaug, he plays a pivotal role in the dragon's demise. Bilbo cracks the riddle to a hidden passageway, allowing him to sneak into Smaug's lair undetected.

Once inside, he tricks Smaug into revealing his underbelly, allowing Bilbo to identify a weak spot in the dragon's scales. This information leads to Smaug's demise, allowing Bilbo and his Dwarven Allies to claim their treasure, albeit briefly.

Shapeshifter: The Elvenking

During Bilbo's journey, his company encounters the Elvenking of Mirkwood forest. It's revealed that the

Dwarves and the Elves have a troubled past, and that the Elvenking disapproves of Dwarves traveling through his woods. He takes the company captive, and Bilbo must free them.

Later, when the Dwarves have reclaimed their treasure, the Elvenking believes that a portion of the gold belongs to him. He's willing to go to war over this dispute.

It's not until the Goblins attack that the Elves and Dwarves realize that they have a common enemy. The Elvenking then reevaluates his priorities and forms an alliance with the Dwarves.

The Elvenking's shifting relationship with Dwarves, and his move from enemy to ally, is typical of a Shapeshifter.

Trickster: Gollum

Gollum is an example of a Trickster, although he diverges a bit from the classic definition.

Gollum does use cunning to try and trick others. He has a desire to eat Bilbo and uses several dastardly ploys to attempt this. He is certainly an "outsider" relative to established societies—even that of the Goblins, which he occasionally preys upon—and survives almost exclusively by his trickery.

However, he's not funny, nor does he use wit to point out the flaws in others. He's actually portrayed as a rather pitiful creature. He does demonstrate one other feature common to many Tricksters: ultimately, his own actions backfire and he ends up defeating himself by trying to be *too* cunning.

Later, in *The Lord of the Rings*, Gollum becomes a better embodiment of the Trickster. His antics come across at times as humorous—alternating with sinister, and occasionally as both simultaneously—and he is constantly at odds with Samwise, whom he calls the "stupid fat hobbit!"

Ally: The Dwarves

Bilbo travels in the company of a band of Dwarves. They act as Bilbo's Allies, and together they face many hardships.

Though their relationship is sometimes strained, by the story's end Bilbo forms a close bond with his traveling companions. When the leader of the group, Thorin, succumbs to the wounds of battle, it brings Bilbo to the point of tears.

It isn't uncommon for a Hero to lose one of his beloved Allies.

Skilled authors can use archetypes to delve deep into the unconscious mind, evoking powerful reactions from the reader.

When assigning your characters to archetypal roles, remember that the archetype doesn't define the character. Archetypes are functions which are filled in the story, and any one character can play multiple roles.

Because they are powerful, archetypal characters are common fixtures in literature. But the danger for writers is in presenting these roles the same way, over and over again. The result is stale, predictable story telling.

The challenge for authors is to re-imagine these archetypes in ways that are fresh and unique. If you take a classic archetype, and put an original spin on it, it retains much of its power while becoming unpredictable and exciting.

The Soul Triptych

The Soul Triptych is a literary mechanism identified by Mr. John Granger, who discovered its use in classic and popular literature.

The Soul Triptych refers to three complimentary characters in a story, with one representing the body, another representing the mind, and a third representing the spirit. As John Granger explained to me in an interview for Mythic Scribes:

> A 'soul triptych' is a story representation of the three powers of soul, which are desires/passions, will/mind, and heart/spirit (what we call "body, mind, and spirit"). This is done via three characters who most aptly represent each and their relationships with the others. For example, Ron, Hermione and Harry, or Gale, Katniss, and Peeta.
>
> It's a trope as old as Plato's charioteer in the *Phaedrus* and as important as the sibling trio in *The Brothers Karamazov*. What makes it so effective is that our reading heart identifies with the heart figure and our soul takes on the

relationship and transformation of its faculties in line with the experience of the characters portrayed.

The body character is usually physically strong, and is driven by his desires or passions. The mind character is the brain of the group. She is often the one who comes up with plans, and demonstrates intellectual prowess. She strives to be driven by clear, rational thinking. The spirit character, in contrast, follows her heart when making decisions.

In recent years, novels that employ these types of trios have been highly successful. Take Harry Potter, for example. Our three main characters are Ron, Hermione, and Harry. Each one of them posses different, yet complementary traits. These differences drive conflict, but also inspire friendship.

The loyal and somewhat simple Ron is the body. The clever and studious Hermione is the mind. And Harry, who always leads with his heart, is the spirit.

A similar trio of characters can be found in *The Hunger Games*, with Gale as the body, Katniss as the mind, and Peeta as the spirit.

The Soul Triptych can be found in all different forms of media. Some examples of body/mind/spirit include:

- Han/Leia/Luke from *Star Wars*

- Gimli/Aragorn/Legolas from *The Lord of the Rings*

- Lion/Scarecrow/Tin Man from *The Wizard of Oz*

- The Thing/Mr. Fantastic/Human Torch (and, increasingly as time went on, Invisible Girl/Woman) from the *Fantastic Four* comics

- And if you'll pardon me for indulging in a little childhood nostalgia, Knuckles/Tails/Sonic from the *Sonic the Hedgehog* video games.

Creating this dynamic between your characters works beautifully when constructing a piece of fiction. The characters are so very different, and yet join perfectly, like pieces of a puzzle.

If you want to use this device in your own novel, my suggestion would be to start with your hero. Ask yourself what he feels most like to you: body, mind, or spirit? Is he tough and hard working? Is he clever and witty? Or is he emotional and free-spirited?

Once you've selected which of these three aspects your Hero embodies, consider the remaining two aspects as you build a pair of Allies. Most uses of the Triptych occur within these archetypes, the Hero and two Allies. That's because this technique is most effective when the three characters form a trio. They must be connected in some way, or work together as a group.

You can experiment with other combinations if you like, such as a Hero, Shapeshifter, and Trickster, each one embodying a different aspect of the Triptych. The vastness of this contrast could lead to interesting scenarios. But the Hero/Ally/Ally combination is the most common.

Further Considerations

Proactive vs. Reactive Protagonists

There are two main types of adventurers: those who go looking for adventure, and those who find it without seeking it out.

The first type is easily kept busy. They may be glory seekers, adrenaline junkies, or possessed of an unconscious (or conscious) death wish. Regardless, they are rarely content unless they're in action. Excellent examples of this type are Conan and Indiana Jones. Others might consider it their duty to repeatedly put themselves in harm's way; Gandalf and Aragorn both qualify.

The second requires more careful handling. These characters constitute the entire rest of the world's population apart from the few who fall into the first type. They're far more realistic—they simply want to live their lives. Depending on the life they want to lead, this may place them in adventurous situations; even then, most would prefer to accomplish their goals in quiet and above all safe fashions.

Which can lead to a major problem for the author: if the character isn't seeking out adventure, how do you get him involved in one? And how do you keep him involved, when in all likelihood all he wants to do is get it over with and go home?

Devices to plunge a character into adventure are innumerable and easily found. Whether it's a wizard showing up on his doorstep, a dying alien handing him a power ring, a marauding army sweeping through his home, or whatever else, the adventure has found the character. He's in, he has no choice, he has to deal with the immediate situation.

But once the immediate situation has been dealt with… then what? If your character is part of that vast majority who prefer safe, stable lives, then logically he'd return to that life. In *The Hobbit*, for instance, Tolkien has no difficulty keeping Bilbo involved during the novel, of course. Which is one of the reasons the quest is such a popular device: the protagonist is separated from his preferred lifestyle, and has no option but to continue until the quest is completed. But once Bilbo returns from his year-long adventure, that's it. He's done. He has no intention of ever leaving home and seeking out trouble again. Nor does he.

This is also true for Frodo in *The Lord of the Rings*. Comparing the two, however, one can see a notable difference between the two protagonists. While at the beginning of his story Bilbo is generally responding to the necessities of his immediate situation, by the end he is a dynamic, self-motivated and highly individualistic agent. He stands in the midst of multiple conflicting forces, and, rather than adhere to any one of them, seeks to resolve their conflicts and bring them into harmony on his own terms.

Frodo, on the other hand, is almost entirely reactive — and is often passive even in his reactions. He's the Ringbearer, which we are repeatedly reminded is a great burden; still, one might wish that this burden weren't so crushing that it prevents him from doing anything other than bearing it. Among the rare instances where he does act on his own are two attempts to "go it alone," when he departs the Shire and when he leaves the party at the Falls of Rauros. Fortunately, he fails in both instances, as success would no doubt have been disastrous. Most of the time, Frodo simply follows whoever he is with, allows them to make the decisions and dictate the action. His most decisive act is when he chooses to accept Gollum as a guide... who he then follows uncritically, slipping back into passive mode yet again.

Of course, Frodo has a vast supporting cast, most of whom are more than sufficiently active to make up for his passivity.

While keeping Frodo largely reactive worked for Tolkien, it's usually best to make your character an active agent in the story. Proactive characters, whose decisions drive the story forward, ultimately make for the most engaging protagonists.

The story-altering decisions that they make will have consequences, not all of which will be positive. In some cases, their decisions may prove to be disastrous for those around them. Seeing how they react to the consequences of their own decisions will provide more opportunities for dramatic, emotional storytelling.

Physical Characteristics

If there's one thing many authors hate, it's giving physical descriptions of characters. How much detail do you provide? How much do you *need* to provide? Which characteristics are important?

The problem is there seems to be only so many physical differences to go around. Eye color? Hair? Skin? Height and weight? Age?

This is only exacerbated if one sticks to real-world ethnic types: apart from Europeans, nearly all of the world has dark hair, for instance; most of these also have dark eyes. The same will apply even if the author creates his own ethnicities: all X have medium-brown hair, green eyes, and sallow skin, for example. Great for allowing characters to readily identify where someone comes from; not so great if the character has to distinguish between individuals of that ethnicity.

In light of this, it becomes truly startling to consider that, in spite of members of any given ethnicity sharing many of these most obvious traits, in the reality of actual contact we experience no difficulty whatsoever in telling one person apart from another. So how to convey this?

There is a simple, if astonishing, answer to the question: *don't*.

I don't mean you should avoid providing physical details for your characters. By all means, any visual details you can give will produce greater depth to your story: this is true for any of its aspects, not merely for the characters. What you should *not* do is worry about giving complete inventories of traits for each character, nor about providing each character with at least one trait that distinguishes her from everyone else in the tale.

If this seems odd, consider that in your story, unlike in the real world, your reader doesn't *need* to be able to distinguish between two characters based on their appearances. Your reader has an easier way to tell your characters apart: their names. Which you'll be using far more often than you will "the green-eyed honey-haired one" and "the blue-eyed russet-haired one."

Which physical details *do* you want to provide? Most writers are tempted to begin with such things as eye and hair color, as I just did above. In fact, these are—at least usually—trivial; as such, we'll get back to them in a bit. No, the ones you want to start with are the ones that help *define the character*... as opposed to what the character *looks* like.

What's the difference? Consider, first of all, that the two descriptions above don't tell you the least thing about the characters involved; all they're good for is picking them out in a tavern, or a lineup. Then consider the following three items, which you will almost always want to provide, or at least hint at, for any character.

Age

This is so important most writers won't even think of it as a "physical" characteristic. The age of a character controls a vast number of other potential traits, ranging from physical ability to education to acquired wisdom to familial and societal status. It's difficult to imagine acquiring a firm sense about a character *without* knowing something about his age. And yet, it's unquestionably physical.

You do not need, nor generally even want, to give a numerical age... though it never hurts to have one in mind (or, better, in your notes). Relative age is usually sufficient: child, youth/adolescent, adult, mature/middle-aged, old, elderly/decrepit. What's important is that the age fit the character, and if it seems not to, that some qualifier be given. A "veteran warrior" might be 40 years old, still more than physically capable of taking the field; if the same warrior is 60, you will probably want to describe him as "yet still hale." Very few "accomplished wizards" are in their twenties, though this will also depend on how you handle magic. The near-term results of dynastic marriages may depend critically on whether either, both or neither of the involved has reached sexual maturity yet.

Build

Height and weight, and the distribution thereof, likewise control a wide range of other possibilities for a character. If she's tall and broad-shouldered, she isn't going to be squeezing through tight passages or lurking in the branches of trees... not well, at least. If she's lanky, she may be great at both of these; if she's slender instead, she may not be able to make it up the tree in the first place. In both cases, being short will benefit the spelunking, though not the climbing, where reach is a virtue. If she's fat, she can probably forget about doing either, regardless of her height.

Which is only the beginning. There are few fat peasants; likewise, there are few waiflike ones. The lifestyle dictates otherwise. There are also few fat message runners or post-riders, for the same reason. Thin innkeepers are rare, skinny eunuchs more so, anorexic sumotori unheard of. Sailors will tend to be strong, but wiry rather than hulking, the latter not being advantageous when scrambling about in rigging. And so on.

Gender

If anything should ever "go without saying," it's that you're going to need to provide this little detail. At least if you're writing about humans. It's also mandatory if you're writing in English and want to use pronouns.

Which can lead to a very enlightening exercise: try writing a story in which you don't use pronouns, and don't identify the genders of the characters in any other way. See what happens.

As with age, this is such a fundamental aspect of the character that most writers won't think of it as a "physical characteristic" in the first place. This is because gender is so heavily freighted with functions, roles and status in real-world society that any *actual* physical differences get overlooked... aside from those involved in procreation. But you're writing your world the way you want it to be: you can, if you wish, throw all that accumulated cultural baggage out. At which point, you're left to establish your own gender relations and roles, and the only factors you absolutely need to take into account are the purely physical ones involved in procreation.

Those are the basics. As mentioned, it's difficult to imagine forming a clear image of a character without all three. From these, we can move on to features that are of a more optional than mandatory nature.

What other possibilities are there? Well, actually... too many to list. Here are some broad categories, with a few specifics mentioned for each. Keep in mind that when selecting features, the goal is not simply to provide an image of the character, but to help define how the character will behave and function within your story.

Actions

A character's kinesics—how he moves his body—can be as telling about him as any other observable physical characteristic. Consider that, in *The Lord of the Rings*, the first important character the hobbits meet on their journey is introduced to them as "Strider." How much do you learn about that character in that one word... that this is such a distinctive part of his being and outward presentation that he is *called* by it, that his "striding" is so distinctive it sets him apart from every other person who goes walking about?

More generally, anyone who's been trained to march in formation will tend to retain the stride length and cadence throughout his lifetime, and can be easily recognized as a soldier, or former soldier, in this way. Likewise, untrained conscripts can be easily recognized for what they are, even when seen individually, because they lack the correct pace features.

Beyond walk, there's also posture, stance, fluidity or awkwardness of some or all motions, and swiftness of reaction. Large characters are often thought of as awkward or clumsy, to such an extent that far too many people are surprised when one turns out not to be. On the other hand, just because someone is an excellent dancer doesn't mean he's any good as a climber... or vice versa. How a character holds his shoulders or distributes his weight while standing still can signal the difference between a peon, a bully, a retired campaigner, and a deadly duellist. And in all likelihood, only the duellist will register the subtleties inherent to each—which is why he's the deadly one.

Gestures and Expressions

You can further enhance a character through recurrent, often unconscious, movements of facial features, hands or body. These range from how—and when, and if—a character smiles or frowns, to tapping or drumming fingers, nail-biting, constantly smoothing or adjusting hair (whether it needs it or not), and so on.

One character might stroke his beard while thinking... or he might do it whenever he has a free hand. Or worse, he might twirl his moustache. Another might always keep her hands folded together when they aren't otherwise engaged, possibly because she has another habit she knows her hands will pursue if she *doesn't* keep them folded.

These may blend with kinesics, where it comes to such things as posture. Does the character sit straight, slouch, rest his head on a fist, sprawl? Can the character sit still, or is he constantly fidgeting, shifting about in his seat?

Facial expressions may be conscious, unconscious or both, and can be excellent indicators of the character's state of mind. Raising an eyebrow, quirking a corner of the mouth up or down, rolling the eyes, shifting the jaw, any number of actions involving the lips... pick a couple, correlate them with internal dispositions, and your readers will be able to see what a character is thinking, without having to be told.

Both this category and the previous one can be affected by culture. Gestures such as nodding or certain hand motions can have different meanings from one culture to another, and even those with similar meanings might be executed differently. Postures might vary depending on the perceived rank of the person being met; demonstrations of respect, such as bowing or saluting, can be even more varied. Looking another person in the eye could be a deadly insult in one culture, whereas not doing so might be in another.

Selecting one or two such features can help flesh out an individual from a distant culture, while at the same time giving a sense of that character's culture in a general way.

Garments and Adornments

This includes everything from clothing to jewelry to cosmetics to hair and beard style to piercings to tattoos and ritual scarification. Many of these will be culturally dependent or circumscribed; others will be available only to those of sufficient wealth. It also includes general cleanliness, fastidiousness and grooming.

How a character approaches cleanliness can create a very distinctive impression. A noble in hiding might adopt peasant clothing, but is he going to adopt a peasant's grime as well?

A character encountered in armor suggests military, of course—but then remember that professional soldiery will have distinct kinesics as well. Your protagonist, or a knowledgeable ally, might recognize an ambush because the "guards" all stand and walk differently. A "common spearman" might have *too* upright and professional a bearing, and thus be revealed as a knight who's put on an infantryman's armor to hide among lesser prisoners.

A common tactic is for a writer to portray a character as vain or feeble by dressing him in imported fabrics colored by imported dyes, decked out in jewelry, painstakingly groomed, and, depending upon age, with dyed hair or a wig. Less often remembered is that such a "feeble" character can easily afford to order a hit on anyone who inconveniences him. Confronting hirsute, unwashed barbarians might prove the safer course in the long run. The point being it is unwise to judge a book by its cover—and that many stereotypes involving dress, grooming and so forth are among the shallowest. True, it's likely the majority of the overdressed, overgroomed, perfumed courtiers will be weak, lazy and decadent. On the other hand, there's nothing about being smelly and poorly-dressed that makes a person formidable, either.

Deformities

Use these sparingly. First off, they tend to become cliché rapidly—just how many people *really* have distinctive birthmarks? Or scars? Keeping in mind that in both cases they have to be someplace visible to matter? Second, many are sufficiently debilitating that it becomes difficult to explain what the character is doing still leading an active, adventurous lifestyle: even scars can cause serious loss of muscular ability, never mind what effects result from twisted limbs, hairlips, hunched backs, or amputations. Don't forget that any noticeable deformity will generally have negative social effects in addition to physical ones.

Along a similar line are such acquired long-term features as calluses, the classic giveaway of the upper-class fugitive trying to hide as a peon. The condition of the teeth can indicate numerous things, including social class, personal hygiene, nutrition, and quality of available medical care, among others. Symptoms of illnesses can be used to expand upon descriptions as well—particularly if they are ones that excite immediate reactions, such as those of leprosy or plague; though less extreme ones such as jaundice, gout and malaria might be more effective if you're planning on keeping the character around for any length of time.

Okay, *now* you're allowed to throw in eye and hair color.

A good idea is to combine mental states with physical actions, using the latter to indicate the former. This is an excellent example of the oft-stated but rarely-explained "show, don't tell" advice. Don't tell your reader that a character is angry: say that she frowns, or glowers, or whatever. *How* she does so, or under what conditions, can then become part of her physically distinctive characteristics... and can vary between similar emotions. When she's disapproving, the corners of her mouth turn down; when she's actively annoyed, her lips thin and her brows narrow; when she's furious, she becomes pale but loses all other facial expression.

Physical Characteristics and Non-Humans

Pretty much, all the above applies regardless of whether a character is human or not. The differences come out in two areas: first, whether any *specific* features apply to a given race; second, how *relative* features apply to a given race.

Specific features are fairly straightforward. In Tolkien's works, for example, all dwarves have beards, almost none of the elves do (those who do may have been oversights), and few hobbits can grow them. Elves have pointed ears. Hobbits have hairy feet.

Scales, feathers, fur, horns, slit pupils, number of fingers/toes... most such items are cosmetic. Ideally, they should not be *purely* cosmetic—this is one criticism that can be leveled against Tolkien: there are no reasons for the differences exhibited by his major races. But whether you give your features functions or not, they're simple enough to apply: all aupiths have crests, for example, some of which are larger than others.

Relative characteristics are another story. The visible expression of such characteristics may not be the same from one race to another: what, for instance, does an old elf or dwarf look like? Does their hair grey and/or thin, do their teeth fall out? At what rate? Similar considerations can be applied to illnesses. Whether or not members of different species can contract or develop the same illness is up to the author... but so are the symptoms of the illness in non-humans.

More importantly, however, are the effects of aging. What does it mean for an elf to be old in the first place? Do they experience diminishing faculties, as humans do? Are they unchanging throughout time?

And how old *is* "old" for an elf? To recur to Tolkien's works again, elves look largely the same throughout most of their lives... and "old" can be old indeed: Galadriel is *at least* 7,185 years old when we encounter her in *The Lord of the Rings*. And she doesn't look a day over thirty. Neither is she any less physically fit than she was when she first came to Middle-Earth. In fact, the only age-related characteristic she has is seven millennia of experience. This is such a formidable difference from the normal "older and wiser" character that it's all but impossible even to grasp.

Dialogue and Speech Patterns

In the real world, one of the most immediate and automatic ways by which we form impressions of others is through speech patterns. Accent, dialect, vocabulary choice, tone, fluidity, even silence: all these and more go into creating first impressions that are generally far stronger than those created by visual cues.

Consider: you encounter a dirty, seam-skinned, bearded man in ragged clothing on a street. He speaks to you in a hesitant, querulous voice, or one slurred as by drink... exactly what you expect; you've got him pigeon-holed. Or he speaks to you confidently, clearly: now what? You begin to wonder if he's what he seems to be. Perhaps he's an undercover cop instead. Even if it turns out he is the homeless beggar he looks like, you're probably that much more likely to give him some assistance, since he "clearly" is not a hopeless degenerate; rather, he's had some bad luck but will return to being a productive member of society just as soon as he gets turned around. Or he speaks with a Harvard—or Oxford—accent, and you're completely thrown: he "must" be a news anchor who, for whatever reason, is doing his own street research.

Here's the problem: when you're writing, you can't capture most of this in dialogue. That is, you can't write the words your characters are saying in such a way that the reader will hear the multitude of nuances which send as many signals as the words themselves.

Nor, for the most part, should you try.

One of the notions beginning writing students find most difficult to shed is that writing ought to reflect the way they speak. (And, conversely, because they know how to speak, they must know how to write as well.) While most of you reading this are beyond that stage, if you have not yet learned this, internalize it now and forevermore: *nobody speaks Standard Written English.* Period. Not the most anal-retentive English teacher, let alone any of the rest of us. Standard Written English is a separate dialect of the English language. Realizing and accepting this can save endless amounts of frustration: once you are aware that this needs to be treated as if it were a different language from the one you speak, it becomes far easier to collate and apply the rules of writing *to* writing, rather than trying to figure out how those rules occur in speech—since many do not.

In everyday speech, shared context makes up an overwhelming component of communication. Shared context is all the things we already know the other person knows, all our mutual past experiences, all the individual past experiences we've spoken to one another of, plus our immediate situation and surroundings. In the real world, two people could be sitting in a restaurant; one gestures toward someone at another table, says a single word—the name of a mutual acquaintance, for example—and both burst out laughing. Both recognize some salient feature shared by their acquaintance and the anonymous diner, one that they find amusing. They manage to recapitulate a complete history of their amusing acquaintance in the course of two communicative signals, taking perhaps two seconds. And if a third person seated at their table wanted to know what's so funny, it would probably take ten minutes to explain.

It gets even worse when we actually *are* talking. The overwhelming majority of speech utterances are *not* complete sentences: most are not even close. Complete sentences appear in monologues: speeches, prepared statements, *very* carefully phrased answers to media questions; they do not appear in actual dialogue. When we converse, fragments are the norm... often highly fragmented fragments. We hesitate, insert unnecessary words, change tracks suddenly, pause in the middle of a thought, talk over one another, finish one another's sentences....

How often have you heard, or been part of, this conversation?

"Did you, uh, hear about John...?"

"Yeah! And she's *such* a—"

"—I know! When she finds out—"

"—gonna... I dunno; don't think she'll—"

"—Can't be*lieve* he—"

"—do... *I* can: he's, like—"

"What I don't get is what she—"

"—y'know? I know what *he*—"

"Yeah. Both of 'em."

Got all that? Good.

To the two people speaking, all this makes perfect sense. They know what they're talking about. If you don't believe that this is the way people normally converse, get yourself a pocket tape recorder, start randomly recording conversations—ideally between others, since your knowledge that you're recording will influence your own utterances—then practice transcribing them... *exactly* as they are spoken. Not only will it convince you that speech in no way resembles writing, you'll discover that accurate transcription of speech is so mind-bogglingly difficult that the conversation above is in fact oversimplified.

If you try writing your dialogue this way, it will be utterly incomprehensible to your readers.

All that's just the words we say: it doesn't include other vocal qualities such as tone, nor does it include expressions, gestures, and so forth. Moreover, when we're talking to one another, we can immediately correct misinterpretations, expand upon points, explain references we mistakenly thought the other was familiar with, clarify, retract, and so on. And do so, constantly. In writing, you don't have those options. What you write has to be able to stand up, now and forever, without additional explanation. This does not mean you can't be *deliberately* vague, mysterious, or oblique... but any information the reader is missing, any confusion of the situation, should be because you intended it, not because the reader can't follow what you're writing.

Writing Dialogue

So, now that you know you aren't going to be able to write your dialogue the way people actually speak, what do you do?

First off, surrender any lingering notion of even attempting to reflect real-world speech. Your characters will speak in complete sentences most if not all of the time. This is a simple necessity to keep your readers from getting lost: it's the same reason the rest of your story is in complete sentences. In the absence of shared context between your characters and your reader, you need to provide a road map for the latter.

That doesn't mean there aren't a considerable number of other options you can use. Not all of them should be applied to every character. Most of your characters will "sound alike," as far as their speech goes; unless you've pulled most of them from a single marginalized group, they will represent the norm against which other variants are judged. Even one or two features can go a long way toward fleshing out the impression a character makes on readers, as well as making her more readily identifiable when she speaks, or if you choose to record internal monologue, when she is thinking.

Vocabulary

This is one of the easiest ones to take advantage of. Some characters have broader vocabularies than others, most often due to education or background. Nor do these words have to be "big" ones, as Glen Cook demonstrates in this exchange from *Lord of the Silent Kingdom*:

"Did he have a story?"

"Fraught with irony."

"I'm surprised you even know two of those three words."

The one speaker is, in fact, ribbing the other, but the point is a good one: not everybody uses the same words.

Also, very few people use all the words they know: *eidolon, pernicious, hubris, cantilever, sobriquet, labyrinthine, embalm, haversack*... some words just tend not to turn up in conversation, not even when they're appropriate. The first speaker above almost certainly would not have believed the second one didn't *know* the words "fraught" and "irony"—that is, he'd expect his friend to recognize and understand the words if he heard them. What was surprising was for the second speaker to make use of them in his own speech.

Characters who persistently use "big" words can include the distracted specialist who keeps forgetting others can't follow his terminology, the politician, priest or con man trying to overwhelm listeners with his rhetoric, or anyone you wish to represent as pompous—especially if he occasionally uses some of the words incorrectly.

Specialized Vocabulary, Jargon

Every profession has its own technical terminology. Steel-clad soldiers have a word for every single piece of metal they're wearing; they also have about twenty terms to describe the various features of a sword, never mind the number of names they have for different kinds of swords. Sailors toss around terms like *larboard*, *lanyard*, *mizzen*, and *points to the wind*.

Nor are all terms unique ones; sometimes, it's a matter of different usage. If an orator throws a retort at you, it's unlikely to cause injury. Whereas if an alchemist throws a retort at you, it would be wise to duck.

Characters can be readily identified, especially upon introduction, by having them employ professional language. They shouldn't do it constantly; they might only do it when they slip up and forget they aren't talking to a fellow professional. The most important thing, if you're going to do this, is to make sure *your* usages are correct. Get them wrong, and neither your characters nor your story will gain credibility.

Magicians are the exception. They may use whatever words you want to invent for them: they are the starship engineers of fantasy, and technobabble is their just and proper domain.

Slang and Colloquial Terms

These work much like jargon in that they are usually the property of a subset of speakers within a larger population. Here, what separates users is not professional need but social factors: class, ethnicity, age, or even neighborhood. None of the non-standard words are technical: all have acceptable standard equivalents. Their function is principally to mark membership in a group—you use the slang of groups you are part of, you don't use the slang of groups you are not. This is a major reason slangs change so rapidly: you can't use your parents' slang without identifying yourself with their generation rather than your own.

Criminal underworlds are notorious for having their own "languages." A few of these words might fall into the "jargon" category, by covering some technical point of the trade. The majority are slang, substituting innocuous terms for incriminating ones.

Using Other Languages

While this can seem like a really nifty thing to do, it rarely adds value to your story. Usually you'll have to translate these passages anyway, in which case the foreign words are just distracting and space-consuming. Or you can leave them untranslated, in which case your readers will either have to choose between remaining in the dark and hoping context will clarify matters, or do the job themselves—assuming you've used a real-world language, say Spanish or Japanese, and assuming they care enough to go to the bother.

That's also assuming you actually wrote the foreign passages correctly in the first place. One all-too-common use of other languages is to have magicians cast their spells in some other language, often Latin. Usually bad Latin, rife with grammatical and other errors. You're better off making up your own words.

And don't even *consider* using a translation program, unless your ambition is to be mocked and derided.

As for making up your own languages: don't bother. Not unless you're planning on devoting a couple years to the task, or are planning on developing it over the course of a vast ongoing series. Even an elementary description of how to go about doing so properly would be as long as this entire book. If you need a few odd words for dramatic effect, make them up as the need arises. Keep notes so that you can use them again; otherwise, leave it at that.

Sentence Structure

Characters of greater education will tend to use more complex sentence forms. Confine your farmers and soldiers, and children (regardless of background), mainly to simple declarative sentences. Allow your professors to spout utterances with multiple subordinate clauses; also permit them greater usage of subjunctives and passive voice. Place artisans, craftsmen, and merchants somewhere in between.

Sentence Length

This one's even easier, though it follows the same pattern. Your brighter, better educated, or more pompous characters won't *always* use long, complex sentences. Those at the other end of the spectrum, however, *never* will. They might produce rambling run-ons made up of individual short sentences strung together, especially when excited or terrified, but it should be easy to see how these could be broken out by replacing their conjunctions with full stops.

Fragments

Yes, we started by trying to eliminate these. Having done so, allowing their deliberate use by a character, as a feature which distinguishes him from all the others speaking in full sentences, can make the character readily recognizable. Perhaps he never uses the pronoun "I" where it would occur in subject position: "Saw them go into the cave. Figured you'd want to know." One excellent, effective and chilling example of frequent fragment usage is the character Rorschach from *Watchmen*.

Dialect Phonetic Features

These are probably the most difficult of the possibilities to handle. First of all, the English alphabet is not designed to accurately represent the sounds of the language: we have twenty-six letters—three of which are completely redundant—to represent upward of forty distinct sounds, depending on dialect. The bigger problem, though, is that few people are trained to recognize which sounds are actually being used when another person speaks. Do you notice each time someone pronounces a word ending with "ng" as though it ended with "n" instead?

As with other features, the basic twofold problem of being accurate and being consistent exists here. On top of these is the complication of needing to invent how to represent your desired sound changes. Using an apostrophe to indicate a dropped sound is simple enough. What to do when you want to indicate an added or changed one is another story. And the farther you get from standard spelling, the harder it will be for the reader to figure out what's being said.

Overall, if a character speaks with a drawl, or a burr, or clips her consonants, or nasalizes her vowels, you're far better off just saying so than trying to represent the sounds.

Dialect Word and Phrasing Features

The brand of English I grew up speaking has a prominent feature which people from other parts of the country notice and remark on: the use of unnecessary prepositions. Whereas people from most of the rest of the English-speaking world would ask "Where is it?" or "Where's he going?" many people from my region ask "Where is it at?" or "Where's he going to?" We can also string together prepositions of location in bewildering ways, from the comparatively benign "up under"—"The cat got up under the chair"—to impossible-to-parse driving directions: "You head on down below the bridge near by the old church, take the right hand fork out around past the lake, and it's up in next to the rail crossing. You can't miss it."

(Note: to be completely reflective of real-world usage, one of these landmarks must no longer exist, e.g. "where the old church used to be.")

Different dialects feature such extraneous expressions as ending declarations with "(so) I did," tacking "you know?" onto a variety of sentence types, or inserting the word "like" in nearly any position whatsoever.

Many American English dialects use "y'all" to indicate second person plural, rather than the standard "you"; other local variants include "youse" or "yinz". Some dialects may freely allow double negatives. A very common feature is not conjugating the verb "to be" for person: "I be, you be, she be," etc. An equally common one is not conjugating *any* verb for third person singular—"she eat/run/talk" rather than "eats/runs/talks."

Similarly, dialects may have unusual words or word-forms, in addition to those already discussed earlier. A quick look at Scots English can provide a number of examples, should they be needed.

Such grammatical features can help to distinguish characters from one another, and are especially useful in prolonged dialogues, as they can give an extra pointer to who's speaking without having to write "X said" one more time. Imagine how easy it would be to track a three-sided conversation where one character says "didn't," a second says "dinna," and the third "din't."

Here you can take a fairly free rein, choosing which words and features you feel like using in your made-up dialect. Which, as usual, you're better off doing than trying to represent a real-world one, as you'll almost inevitably fail to get it right. And again, as with all other linguistic features, you need to be able to use these consistently... a bit more so, since these will stand out more prominently than vocabulary choice or sentence length. There is little that can make your dialogue less plausible than to have a character use "agin" for "against" on one page, then not use it two pages later.

Conclusion: Pulling It All Together

When building a character, the first layer is your character's foundation: the unconscious mind. To help define his inner workings, you can use the Enneagram to select a generalized type that will drive your character's actions.

The second layer is how your character fits into his own world. This includes how he interacts with others, as well as his social status and responsibilities. The Bartle Types and Five Great Relationships can help to delineate these aspects of the character.

The third and final layer is your character's place within your story. He has a role to fill, which can be labeled as an archetype. You may also use the Soul Triptych to add another dimension to your character and two of his relationships.

These layers can be approached separately in order to help create a compelling character. Ideally, though, they should be approached in unison, enabling you to construct a fleshed-out character from the ground up.

Bringing all three layers together can appear daunting, but will seem natural once you get started.

Remember that neither your character nor your story is written in stone while still in production. If your character doesn't feel right, you can go back at any time and do some restructuring. The first draft of anything, including a character worksheet, will need multiple revisions. That comes with the territory of writing.

One of the benefits of using this method is that it can help minimalize backtracking. If you have the most detailed image possible of who your character is from the beginning, you won't find yourself having to go back and alter his actions all the time. It will still happen from time to time, but you can minimalize the need for it.

If you're having trouble getting the layers to connect, you can gain a better understanding of the Enneagram and the Bartle Types by taking the tests for yourself. Looking at yourself in terms of these classifications will help you to see how the first and second layers connect.

When building a character, it should be noted that the layers will not always fit together neatly. For some characters, all three layers will align in a logical sequence. For others, the layers will show great contrast, or will appear contradictory. There are advantages and disadvantages to both outcomes.

Characters whose three layers don't fit neatly together can be unique and interesting. One example is Claude Frollo from *The Hunchback of Notre-Dame*. The contradictions between his three layers are what make him a memorable villain. His unconscious mind is driven by desire and impulses, classifying him as a Romantic in his first layer. In his second layer, his role in society is that of a holy man, and he has a responsibility to uphold morality. In his third layer, he fits the role of the Shadow within the plotline. So what we end up with is a highly emotional, religious, dark villain. These layers contrast sharply, and make for a complex character.

But it is challenging to write a character who is highly complex. If you're having difficulty making the three layers come together within a character, it becomes even harder if each layer contrasts with the others. If done carelessly, the character may seem more weird than interesting, as if he's making odd decisions for no reason.

A character whose layers are in conflict can also be controversial. Portraying a religious man as a villain, as is the case with Claude Frollo, proved unsettling to some people. When Disney made an animated film adaptation of *The Hunchback of Notre-Dame*, they changed Frollo's second layer, so that his role in society was that of a judge. This maintained some of the contrast, but lessened the chances of a backlash.

Constructing a character whose three layers match has its own set of pros and cons. A character whose layers complement one another can be a good starting place for an aspiring novelist, as such characters are less complex. At the same time, such characters may be less unique and interesting. They can even come across as two-dimensional and predictable.

This outcome can be avoided. Not every character with matching layers is boring. Vito Corleone, whom I've mentioned before, is a great example of this. In his first layer, he's an Achiever who is driven by success. In his second layer, his place in society reflects his level of achievement, and he has a high social status—as well as the accompanying responsibilities. And in his third layer, his success enables him to be a highly effective Mentor.

Even though all three of his layers fit together smoothly, he's still a memorable character because of how Mario Puzo writes him. Rather than depicting this criminal overlord as a violent thug, Puzo makes him an intelligent, cultured, and sympathetic family man. Vito uses his success to provide for his family, and to care for poor Italian immigrants. Showing this criminal to be a human being makes him a compelling character, even though his layers aren't in conflict.

So when writing a character whose layers match, avoid predictability. And when building a character whose layers contrast, be wary of choices that may appear as pointless oddities. Do this, and you'll minimize the cons of both approaches to layered structuring.

This layered approach to character building can lead to a better story. Meticulously building your characters, layer by layer, will require a greater investment of time. But your end product will be so much richer for having done so. The hard work of character building doesn't go unrewarded.

Once you have developed your character's layers, you can move on to other important considerations, such as disposition (proactive vs. reactive), physical characteristics, and use of spoken language.

It will take practice to master the strategies in this book, but writing has always been about practice. Few authors produce anything worth reading without first toiling through years of practice. Don't let the complexity of this approach intimidate you. Just dive in, and it will be easier than you think.

Writing is a calling. It's about crafting stories that move readers. Creating characters is just one aspect of this. This book can show you ways to write characters, but only you can put the pen to the paper. If you want to write, pursue your passion. If you have the calling, answer it.

Remember—writers write. They don't just dream of writing, they don't plan to write someday, they don't wait for the muse to strike them.

They write.

Character Worksheet

A printer-friendly version of this worksheet can be downloaded from

http://mythicscribes.com/character-worksheet/

Preliminary Info:

- Character's full name:

- Nickname or alias:

- Reason for nickname or alias:

- Race or ethnic group:

- Occupation:

- Education or training:

- Financial situation:

- What is the character's long-term goal for his or her life?

- What is the character's immediate goal, which is his or her primary objective in the story?

- How are the character's long-term and immediate goals connected?

LAYER I: THE CHARACTER WITHIN

The first and deepest layer is the character's unconscious mind, which forms the basis of his actions and motivations.

1.1 The Unconscious Mind

The unconscious mind holds memories, drives and instincts that are deep within the character. The unconscious mind will often drive a character's decisions, even if the character is unaware of this fact.

- What is the character's primal fear?

- What is the source of this fear?

- What is the character's most vivid childhood memory?

- What is the character's most painful memory?

- How do these memories influence the character's decisions?

1.2 The Enneagram

The enneagram classifies individuals into nine categories based on their unconscious drives and motivations. It offers a rudimentary template of who they are, and therefore how they will likely act.

Personality Type

- Which personality type best describes the character?
- How does the character fit the description of this personality type?

Strengths and Their Impact:

- What are the strengths of the character's personality type?
- In what ways does the character demonstrate these strengths?
- How have these strengths impacted the character's past?

Weaknesses and Their Impact:

- What are the weaknesses of the character's personality type?
- In what ways does the character demonstrate these weaknesses?
- How have these weaknesses impacted the character's past?
- What is the character's deepest secret?
- What does the character fear happening if the secret is revealed?
- Who knows the secret already?
- What is the character's biggest regret?
- What is the character's critical flaw?

- How is this flaw introduced to the readers?

- How does this flaw influence the course of the story?

Influences:

- How does the character's personality type influence his or her spirituality?

LAYER II: THE CHARACTER IN HIS OR HER WORLD

The second layer is how the character relates to his or her world. This includes how the character approaches the world, and the character's formative relationships.

2.1 Bartle Types

Bartle Types are about interaction. Bartle Types classify how characters interact with their environment, and how they interact with others.

Bartle Type

- Which Bartle type best describes how your character approaches the world and others?

Interactions with the World

- How does the character approach the world?

- How does the character's Bartle type influence his or her hobbies?

- How does the character react to extreme stress?

Interactions with Others

- What is the character's general behavior towards other?

- How does the character show affection?

- Describe the character's sense of humor:

- Does the character get jealous easily?

- Does the character seek to please others?

- When interacting with others, is the character primarily honest or dishonest?

2.2 The Five Great Relationships

There are five main relationships in our lives that shape us as people. A character's relationships determines his responsibilities, as well as his social status. Relationships can limit what is possible, but can also open new possibilities, and are rich sources of conflict.

1. Ruler and Subject (Government)

- How does the character view authority figures?

- What does the character think about the role of government?

- In what nation and city was the character born?

- Describe the character's current relationship with the government of his or her birthplace:

- In what nation and city does the character currently live?

- Describe the character's relationship with the government of his or her current residence:

2. Parents and Child

- Names, ages, and occupations of the character's parents:

- Describe the character's relationship with his or her mother:

- Describe the character's relationship with his or her father:

- Does the character have any children?

- If so, list their names and ages:

- Describe the character's relationship with each child:

3. Husband and Wife (Romance)

- Name and describe the character's primary spouse or lover:

- What is the nature of the character's commitment to his or her spouse/lover?

- Is the character involved in any secondary, clandestine or adulterous relationships?

- If so, describe these relationships:

- Describe any significant past relationships:

4. Elder Sibling and Younger Sibling

- Does the character have any siblings?

- If so, list their names and ages:

- Describe the character's relationship with each sibling:

- What is the character's birth order?

- How did the character's birth order impact him or her?

5. Friend and Friend

- Name and describe the character's most significant friend(s):

- How did the character meet his or her closest friend(s)?

- Does the character prefer to have many or few friends?

- Other significant relationships:

LAYER III: THE CHARACTER IN YOUR STORY

The third and final layer is the character's role in your story. This layer can be developed using mythological archetypes, as well as a concept known as the Soul Triptych.

3.1 Archetypes

Archetypes are recognized roles that your characters can step into, and are rooted in the collective unconscious of all human beings. They are functions which are filled in the story, and any one character can play multiple roles.

<u>Role</u>

- Which archetype best describes the character's function in the story?
- What makes the character well-suited to perform this function?

3.2 Soul Triptych

The Soul Triptych is a literary mechanism that consists of three complimentary characters in a story, with one representing the body, another representing the mind, and a third representing the spirit.

- Is the character part of a soul triptych?

- If so, which aspect does the character represent (Body, Mind, or Spirit)?

- In what ways does the character embody this aspect?

- Who are the other two characters in the triptych, and which aspects do they represent?

FURTHER CONSIDERATIONS

Proactive vs. Reactive Protagonists

- Is this character a protagonist in your story?

- If so, offer an example of the character making a decision that alters the course of the story.

- How does this decision impact other characters, especially those closest to the protagonist?

Physical Characteristics

Don't worry about giving complete inventories of traits for your character. Rather, focus on the traits that help *define the character*, as opposed to what the character *looks* like.

1. <u>Age and Health:</u>
   - Character's biological age:
   - Does the character appear younger or older than his or her biological age?
   - If so, what is the reason for this discrepancy?
   - Health Concerns:

2. <u>Build:</u>
   - Body type or build:
   - Height:
   - Weight:
   - How does the character feel about his or her height and weight?

3. <u>Gender:</u>
   - Is the character biologically male or female?
   - Does the character self-identify as male or female?

4. <u>Actions:</u>
   - How does the character walk?
   - Describe the character's posture:
   - Does the character move quickly or slowly?
   - Is the character dexterous or clumsy?

5. Gestures and Expressions:

- What are some of the character's most used gestures?

- Does the character have any distinctive mannerisms or quirks?

- Does the character routinely perform any unconscious movements?

- What are the character's most used facial expressions?

6. Garments and Adornments:

- Cleanliness:

- Style of dress:

- Body art and jewelry:

- Does the character wish to stand out, or blend in?

7. Deformities:

- Does the character have any visible scars or injuries?

- If so, how did he or she obtain them?

- Was the character born with any deformities?

8. Other details:

- Complexion:

- Skin texture:

- Hair color:

- Hair length and style:

- Eye color:

- Most striking feature:

- Other distinguishing features:

- What would the character most like to change about his or her appearance?

Dialogue and Speech Patterns

Most of your characters will "sound alike," as far as their speech goes; unless you've pulled most of them from a single marginalized group, they will represent the norm against which other variants are judged. Therefore, even one or two distinguishing features can go a long way toward fleshing out the impression a character makes on readers, as well as making her more readily identifiable when she speaks.

1. Spoken Language

- Primary spoken language:

- Secondary spoken language(s):

- Describe the character's speaking voice:

- Is the character's speech slow, fast, or moderate?

2. Vocabulary and Dialect

- Describe the character's vocabulary and use of language:

- Does the character speak with a regional dialect or accent?

Additional Reading

Richard Bartle. *Designing Virtual Worlds*. New Riders, 2003.

Joseph Campbell. *The Hero with a Thousand Faces*. New World Library, 2008.

James N. Frey. *The Key: How to Write Damn Good Fiction Using the Power of Myth*. St. Martin's Griffin, 2002.

John Granger. *How Harry Cast His Spell*. Tyndale Momentum, 2008.

Helen Palmer. *The Enneagram: Understanding Yourself and the Others in Your Life*. HarperOne, 1991.

Laurie Schnebly. *Believable Characters: Creating with Enneagrams*. Cider Press, 2010.

Christopher Vogler. *The Writer's Journey: Mythic Structure for Writers*. Michael Wiese Productions, 2007.

About Antonio del Drago

Antonio del Drago, Ph.D., is the founder of Mythic Scribes, an online community of fantasy writers and fans. When he isn't writing speculative fiction, he works as a professor and non-fiction author.

Antonio's favorite authors include J.R.R. Tolkien, C.S. Lewis, Alexandre Dumas, James Fenimore Cooper, Robert E. Howard, J.K. Rowling, and Patrick Rothfuss.

About Mythic Scribes

Mythic Scribes is a community of fantasy writers who are passionate about storytelling. We provide a platform for new and aspiring authors, as well as a meeting place for writers and fans of the genre.

Founded in 2011, Mythic Scribes has grown into a thriving community of both professional and amateur writers. Among its standout features are a writing showcase, where authors can share their work and request feedback. There also are forums dedicated to world building, writing questions, publishing, book promotion, and book cover design.

Mythic Scribes has become one of the leading destinations online for those committed to the art of fantasy writing. We invite you to become a part of our growing community of writers.

Visit us today at mythicscribes.com

CPSIA information can be obtained at www.ICGtesting.com
Printed in the USA
LVOW081308230413

330523LV00001B/44/P